THE DOGS WHO PLAY BASEBALL

Thomas Louis Carroll

ISBN: 978-1-7366339-3-9 Paperback
     978-1-7366339-2-2 Ebook

Editor: Margaret A. Harrell, https://margaretharrell.com
Cover designer: Laura Chambliss of StudioYopp.com

 To contact the author about speaking appearances and/or signed copies and bulk orders, go to www.DogsWhoPlayBaseball.com

ALMANOR
& LORAQUE
PRESS

Almanor & Loraque Press, Inc.
300 Central Avenue SW
Suite 2000 East
Albuquerque, NM 87102

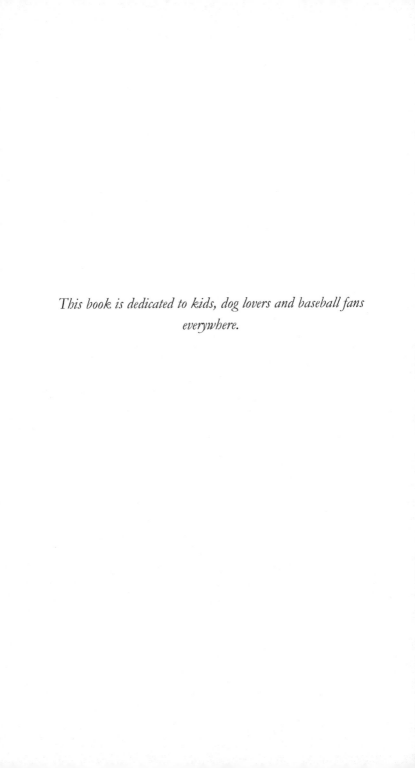

This book is dedicated to kids, dog lovers and baseball fans everywhere.

There are two things Americans love—dogs and baseball, and we have both.

—Louie Cohen,
third baseman for the Bronx Badgers

CONTENTS

Chapter One: THE BRONX BADGERS 9

Chapter Two: A DOCTOR IN QUEENS 29

Chapter Three: THE SEEING EYE DOG 35

Chapter Four: FINDING A WAY.....................................44

Chapter Five: MAKING LEMONADE.............................49

Chapter Six: TOUCHING THIRD BASE 57

Chapter Seven: THEY CAN PLAY! 64

Chapter Eight: FLING BALL 71

Chapter Nine: THE DOGS WHO PLAY BASEBALL 83

Chapter Ten: THE RENT 96

Chapter Eleven: HEY KID, GOT AN AGENT?............. 106

Chapter Twelve: MAGGIE HART 111

Chapter Thirteen: GREATEST PLACE ON EARTH 118

Chapter Fourteen: DOGS DON'T PLAY BASEBALL....125

Chapter Fifteen: FRONT PAGE STORY........................ 140

Chapter Sixteen: NO BARKING IN BASEBALL 144

Chapter Seventeen: SMILE ON A SUMMER EVE........ 164

Chapter Eighteen: THE RING...171

Chapter Nineteen: FLOWERS EVERYWHERE 177

Chapter Twenty: GET YOUR HOT DOGS.....................181

Chapter Twenty-One: DOGS AND BASEBALL 187

Chapter Twenty-Two: THE PRESS CONFERENCE ... 195

Chapter Twenty-Three: ON THEIN 205

Chapter Twenty-Four: BACK ON THE PROWL........... 212

Chapter Twenty-Five: FREDDY THE LITTLE BOY ... 217

Chapter Twenty-Six: THE BIG GAME 226

Chapter Twenty-Seven: CHESTER'S AUTOGRAPH.... 257

Chapter Twenty-Eight: THE VISITOR........................... 260

ACKNOWLEDGMENTS 263

ABOUT THE AUTHOR 265

Chapter One
THE BRONX BADGERS

Louie Cohen swung. With a crack of the bat, the ball flew upwards, rising higher and higher into the sky over the ballfield in the Bronx, pausing for a moment at the top of its arc, and then plummeting downwards in a blur. Just a moment before it hit the outfield grass, a set of jaws reached out, lunged for it, nabbed it, and hauled it in.

"Nice catch, boy," Louie called to his white Labrador, Chester. The dog had a friendly face, a hard, athletic body, powerful legs, large paws that grabbed the turf as he ran, and quick eyes. "Okay, bring it in."

Chester turned around and ran the ball in, stopping a few feet away and rolling it back to Louie. Since the day he was born eight years ago, Chester had been Louie's dog. He went everywhere with Louie, especially to the ballfield every summer afternoon, where he shagged flies with the best of them.

"He could play first base for us," said a girl's voice behind Louie.

"What about third?" Louie said.

Sally smiled. "Yeah, right, we need a good third baseman." She was kidding, of course, because Louie was their third baseman, and many said he had the strongest throw to first of any fifth grader in all of New York City. Sally lounged on the infield grass with her dog Marmalade, a lean grey Whippet who sniffed the grass with her long, spotted nose while making quick back and forth movements of her head.

"Grounder," Louie said. Once he heard that, Chester ran out to shortstop and turned around. Louie hit a hard ground ball in the hole. Like a shot, Chester raced to the ball, got in front of it, knocked it down with his chest, and grabbed it in his mouth.

"Just like Dexter Archer," said Sally.

"Oh, Chester could have taken Archer's place when he retired," said Louie. "They just don't let dogs play baseball."

"True that," she said, as Marmalade rested her head on Sally's legs. She and Louie had been friends for, well, since before either of them could remember—growing up in the same neighborhood, going to the same school, and playing on the Bronx Badgers together.

"Right here, boy," Louie said. Chester ran the ball in, halting a few feet away. With the ball firmly held in his mouth, the dog dropped his head and flung the ball up in a perfect toss right into Louie's outstretched hand.

"Nice flip," said Sally. "Maybe he could pitch."

"Yeah, we could sure use some pitching," said Louie, chuckling because Sally was the star pitcher of their team.

"Okay, boy, Archer's up," Louie said. Chester instantly got into his dog crouch—legs ready to run, and he was off before Louie hit the ball.

Louie called it in his announcer voice. "*It's a fly ball down the left field line off the bat of Dexter Archer. Archer rounds first and heads for second. Chester has a play on it. He's back and back and back, to the wall. He leaps . . . He's got it! Dexter Archer robbed of a home run after a great catch by Chester.*"

"Archer's retired," said Sally, matter-of-factly.

"Yeah, but he's still Archer, he'll always be Archer," said Louie. Chester came barreling back, breathing hard, the ball in his mouth.

"You took a homer away from Dexter Archer," said Sally. "Way to go." Chester dropped the ball and barked, a single loud bark.

"You can say that again," said Louie and Sally together.

Louie yanked the brim of his Yankees cap. Since this was the Bronx, a borough of New York City, that meant it was Yankees country. *The New York Yankees*— the boys in pinstripes—with that world-renowned "NY" logo on the shirt. With the dark blue hats. And dark socks starting just below the knee, extending down to the blue-and-white cleats. These were not normal baseball players—they were the descendants of Babe Ruth, Lou Gehrig, Mickey Mantle, Mariano Rivera, and the greatest Yankees shortstop ever—Dexter Archer. They were not just players. They were heroes.

And the stadium, not just any stadium, but the world-famous *Yankee Stadium*, was just a short bike ride away from where they were right now—just down Grand Concourse Avenue. It was the cathedral of baseball, the place where the gods resided, the field every boy and girl in New York wanted to play on. It was, in short, a field of glory. When you approached the outside of the stadium, the first thing you saw were the towering white walls with the curved arches. The magnificent white marble walls climbed to the heavens, and if you stood underneath, you could feel the power of the stadium. It spoke to you—saying, *you are standing in a place of honor, a place of baseball history, a place of magical moments, so don't you forget it, kid. Don't ever forget it.*

If you looked up at Gate Four, you could barely make out in yellow lettering YANKEE STADIUM at the top of the arches, below the flags flying at the top of the wall. Looking to the left and the right, the stadium curved away from you, as if it went on forever. You could not even stand in the shadow of the stadium without realizing that there was something going on here. For *here* they played the greatest game on earth, and if you could just get in past these massive walls, you could see the game in action. Because inside the stadium, it got even better.

Never in the history of the world has there been anything as green as That Field. The grass almost hurt your eyes, it was so green. The groundskeepers mowed it into perfect rows of grass, crossing diagonally. The infield had small rows, the outfield wider rows, every blade perfectly cut, and evenly topped off. It was as if someone had measured each blade of grass and cut it lovingly. The pitcher's mound rose like a dirt wave rushing towards the shore. The infield between the bases cut a brown diamond into the grass. The infield between the bases had the finest brown dirt, raked smooth to stop bad hops. It was on this infield that the mighty Yankees fielded the ground balls and ran the bases.

Behind the batter's box was the high wire screen to catch foul balls, rising almost to the second level of seats. And in the outfield, past the warning track, rose the wall. And behind that, the bleachers, where the bums hung out—the guys with big stomachs who drank too much beer and hurled swear words down onto the field. It got rowdy up there, especially a few dozen rows back. Guys threw beer and bags of peanuts. Drunks hollered. To get the hot dogs to the customers, the vendors threw the hot dogs wrapped in silver foil over forty rows of spectators. It was a rough place to watch a game, and Louie and Sally loved every minute of it.

Louie and Sally had sat in the bleachers at games with Louie's dad maybe three hundred, four hundred times. They'd seen Archer dive for a ball in the hole, come up with it, and nail the runner at first by a step. They'd seen the greatest relief pitcher of all time, Mariano Rivera, strike out the side again and again. They'd seen the Yankees come from behind in the ninth and win with a walk-off home run. And on the way out of the park, their shirts stained with mustard from their hot dogs, they'd pass statues of Babe Ruth, Lou Gehrig, and other Yankee greats. This was Yankee Stadium, right down the street from where they were right now.

You couldn't live here—not in this neighborhood, not around here—and be a Mets fan, or a Phillies fan, or worst of all, a Red Sox fan. You'd be taking your life into your hands. They'd run you out of town. They'd revoke your Bronx citizenship. They'd string you up. You had to be a Yankees fan—you had to be! And, so, they were.

But today the Yankees were on the road in Cleveland. So it was time for *their* game, the Bronx Badgers—Louie's and Sally's team. Sally started warming up, throwing the ball back and forth as Chester and Marmalade scampered around. Sally wore her Yankees cap turned backwards, so the back strip crossed her freckled forehead. She had the oldest, most raggedy mitt you ever saw; it looked like it would come apart at any minute. But Sally had used it for years to snag come-backers to the mound, and she wouldn't give it up.

Something about Louie and Sally said *baseball*. Even without their hats and beat-up gloves, their Louisville Sluggers with marks on the bat for every home run, and the raggedy baseballs, people knew they were baseball kids.

"What position do you play?" people would ask.

"Third," said Louie.

"Pitcher," said Sally.

Louie always wore his hat with the bill facing front. He was tall for his age, lean, with dark hair parted on the side, a strong right arm to throw runners out, strong legs to beat out a slow roller up the line, and good eyes to see a fastball on the inside corner. And though no one could see it, the strong beating heart of a baseball player.

Sally was tall, very tall. A tomboy, people said, with her hair in two braids all the time, sweet-faced, with loads of freckles, usually wearing jeans and tee-shirts. She had that athletic confidence scouts looked for. She moved gracefully, and her pitching arm was strong. Just what you needed to pitch for the Badgers in the Bronx Little League division.

"You still sleep with your glove under your pillow?" asked Louie, whipping back the ball.

"Yeah, I guess," she replied, hauling it in.

"Me too, but don't tell anyone. We're in fifth grade, after all."

Sally threw back high, Louie jumped, it sailed over his head, and Chester raced across the infield after it. Marmalade jumped up and beat Chester to it; they ran into right field together.

"Chester may be able to catch the ball, but he'll never catch Marmalade," said Sally.

The other players started to arrive. "They're here, come on," said Louie.

Sally and Louie made their way over to the dugout, where the rest of the team was pulling gear out of duffel bags, arranging the bats against the fence, wiping off the batting helmets caked with yesterday's mud, and tossing out the hardballs for the warmup. The ballfield at Van Cortland Park had a rough grass infield and a spotty grass outfield with gopher holes every twenty yards or so that they had to watch out for. Behind home plate, the backstop teetered and swayed. There were two dirt-floor dugouts, beat-up bases, and the remnants of white lines running up both base lines, gradually disappearing in the outfield.

For today's game they had nine players, and everyone brought their dogs. There was hot-headed Chip with his Great Dane named Pal, nervous-Nellie Juan with his German Shepherd Oscar, sass-monster Cara with her mutt Donut, and stocky Ron with his Bernese Mountain Dog Bernie.

"Who's ready to play some *baseball?*" yelled Sally.

There was chunky Chuck with his Bulldog named Bull, baby-faced Levar with his Collie named Champ, feisty Veronica with her Bassett Hound Gabby, and daffy Donna with her Scotty named Pearl. Together, along with Louie and Sally, and Chester and Marmalade, they made up the Bronx Badgers and their dogs who showed up at every game.

Today's game was against the One Hundred Ninety-fifth Street Cougars, who were slowly taking up residence in the opposing dugout, in their white uniforms with *Cougars* on the front—although the printer had placed the name too far to one side of their shirts so only the "Coug" was showing. But no one cared. It was baseball that mattered.

"Look, it's Mr. Park," yelled the kids as a man approached. He had a round face, a great big smile, chubby arms, and an apron that bore the logo of MR. PARK'S MARKET. Across from the baseball field was a row of shops, and Mr. Park owned one, a Korean grocery market. He was carrying a brown bag, like he did most game days.

"Big game today," he called out. "Big game needs big snack." He reached into his bag and brought out oranges, cashews, almonds, raisins, and crackers—and handed them out to the kids, who dug in.

"Thank you, Mr. Park," yelled the kids.

"Oh, very good, very good," he replied.

Louie reached into his pocket and pulled out a ten-dollar bill. "My mother wanted you to have this," he said. Mr. Park waved it away. "You no pay, you play, you play. Get it? No pay, you play," he said with a laugh.

"Yes, we get it," said Sally, rolling her eyes.

"Okay, now for dogs," said Mr. Park. "Dogs line up."

The kids knew just what to do. They formed a line on one side and lined the dogs up about five feet away across from them. The dogs, sensing a treat coming, kept perfectly still. Holding the brown grocery bag, Mr. Park walked slowly between the two lines, handing out one dog biscuit to each kid. When he got to the end, he turned and yelled "Now." The kids whipped their dog biscuits at the dogs, and the dogs, standing on their hind legs, expertly caught them in their mouths and chewed them up.

"Oh, dogs are good, dogs very good," said Mr. Park, smiling broadly, very pleased with himself, as the dogs munched happily.

Mr. Park headed back to his store. "Good luck today."

"Bye, Mr. Park. Thank you," yelled the kids. "Thank you."

"Okay, bring it in," said Louie. The kids gathered around Sally and Louie, holding their dogs by their collars.

"Cara, how's Donut's paw?"

"Cut's all better." She held up Donut's paw and they all crowded around. She was a funny-looking thing, a mutt's mutt, with brown ears that pointed straight up and turned left and right when she thought she heard a cat; a thin, bony body, and a head that flitted back and forth.

"How about Oscar?"

"His leg's still hurt," said Juan. "I wrapped it again last night."

"Okay, take it easy with him today," ordered Louie. "And what about Pearl?"

Donna lifted Pearl up and put her down on the picnic table. "They pulled her tooth," she said and the kids pushed forward to get a look. "I don't think it hurts anymore, but it sure looks funny. See?" She pulled back her dog's lip and the kids marveled at the missing tooth. "Whoaaaaaa," they said, wide-eyed.

"Look what Bull can do." Chuck carried Bull the Bulldog to third, put him down and whistled. Bull immediately raced for home. Chuck whistled again and Bull threw all four legs out and slid across home plate on his belly.

"I'd say *safe*," said Sally. "Right? Safe."

"Okay, put 'em in the dugout," said Louie.

The kids hustled their dogs into the dugout and put them in a *sit-stay* before heading out onto the field for the first inning. Pearl the Scotty whined, because she wanted to go out there with them, so Donna ran back and gave her a kiss.

"Sorry, dogs don't play baseball," she said, hugging her. "You know that."

"Juan, aren't you're forgetting something?" said Louie.

"Oh, yeah." Juan ran to his bag, pulled out a roll of tape, and climbed up the backstop fence to the sign ten feet up that read: NO DOGS ALLOWED. Pulling tape off the roll, he placed it in strips over the letter N and O until the NO disappeared. Then, it read: DOGS ALLOWED.

"Good, now we can play," said Louie.

Sally headed to the mound, Louie to third base, and the rest of the players to their positions. The Cougars came up to bat. "Easy out," said Louie from third as the lead-off hitter stepped into the batter's box. Sally looked in for the sign from the catcher, straightened, wound up, and threw a fastball.

"Ball," yelled the umpire.

"Caught the corner," Sally yelled back.

"Ball," grumbled the ump.

"Chester?" yelled Sally.

Chester barked.

"See?" said Sally.

Her next pitch hung over the plate. Waiting on it, the Cougar batter hit a screaming line drive over the first baseman's head into right field, and it rolled all the way to the fence. Juan, in right field, went for it, but the dogs, watching the ball go by, couldn't stop themselves and took off into right field after it.

"Oh, brother," wailed Louie. "Get them off the field."

Juan managed to wrestle the ball from Gabby and threw to second. The Cougar slid into second just ahead of the tag. Then the game had to stop while Louie and his teammates rounded up the dogs and yanked them back to the dugout.

"Sorry," said Louie to the Cougars.

"Louie, look."

Louie turned to see. Walking towards them was a whole team of kids, older kids. Carrying bats and catcher's gear, they were tossing balls up and slapping their gloves. At the head of the gang was a red-haired kid. His big mouth, over floppy lips, barely covered his jagged teeth.

"It's Froggy," said Sally.

"What does *he* want?"

Froggy's real name wasn't Froggy. It was Frank or Fran or something like that. Everyone just called him Froggy, though, even his friends. Even his *mother*. Froggy had a face that his mother could love, but nobody else. When he scrunched it up, he looked like one of those mirrors at the amusement park, which might be why people called him Froggy. Nobody knew.

"What do you want, Froggy?"

"Off," ordered Froggy, waving his arm.

"This is our field," said Louie. "We've got it."

"Yeah, well, we want it."

"Didn't you hear? We got it," said Sally.

"You *had* it. And now we got it," said Froggy.

"Look, Froggy," said Sally, "I know you have limited intelligence, and I don't mind, really I don't, because somebody has to be at the low end of the IQ scale, but as even you can see, we got the field."

"So get off."

"We're getting off, like you're getting pretty," she snapped back.

"Okay, if you don't get off, we're gonna take it, so I'm going to count to ten and—"

"You can count?" exclaimed Sally. "I had no idea."

"One, two, three—"

"Four is next," said Sally, "in case you forgot."

"Four, five, six—"

"You've done a lot of good work, Froggy. You should be very proud," she said.

"Seven, eight—"

"All the way to eight. My, my."

"Nine, ten. Okay, take it," said Froggy, and with that his team rushed the Badgers. Froggy reached for Louie's neck. And in no time Froggy and his team had all of them on the ground or up against the backstop.

And then—Chester growled. And all the other dogs growled, low and mean. Froggy stopped, frozen in his tracks.

"Good move, Einstein," sneered Sally.

"They won't do anything," said Froggy to his friends, and he wrapped his hands around Louie's throat and raised his fist. Chester lunged forward until he was inches from Froggy's leg, barking ferociously and baring his teeth.

"I wouldn't do that if I were you," warned Sally. "If I give the command…"

"You wouldn't."

"Try me," said Sally.

The dogs, showing teeth, waited for the command to attack. Froggy looked at Chester, then at the other dogs—all growling, ready to pounce.

"Take a walk," yelled Sally.

Froggy looked around at the growling dogs, then snuck a look at his nervous teammates, shook his head, let go of Louie, stepped back, and said, "Oh, forget it." His teammates let go of the Badgers. He led them off the field.

"And don't come back," yelled Sally after them.

Froggy whipped around and shook his fist.

"Whoaaaaa," yelled back the Badgers.

"This isn't over, you know. We'll be back," said Froggy.

"Come back, and we'll work on your numbers," said Sally. "Eleven is next."

Froggy fumed, his face red as a St. Louis Cardinals hat.

"Get off our field," yelled Cara.

"Yeah, and stay off," everyone yelled at once.

Froggy turned his back on them and walked away. Sally watched them leave the field. "He'll be back, you know," she said. Louie just shrugged. "Okay, who's up?"

They played a good seven-inning game before they had to give up the field at four o'clock to the local high school team, the Red Cats of Bronx P.S. 171. Having gathered up their dogs—Donut and Pearl and Bull and all the others—they slapped gloves with the arriving high schoolers, threw all their equipment, the bats and ragged hardballs, catcher's gear, and the bases, into duffel bags and headed out, a caravan of kids and dogs and bags and bats and gloves. They walked past Mr. Park's market.

"You win today?" asked Mr. Park, outside sweeping.

"Five to three," said Louie.

"That good, that very good. See you tomorrow," Mr. Park said, holding his broom to his chest. "Bye, Louie. Bye, Sally. Bye, Chester." Chester barked. Mr. Park laughed. "Chester say goodbye, too. Bye, Chester."

On the way home, as they always did, they rode their bikes past Yankee Stadium and stopped in front of the main entrance, on Babe Ruth Plaza. They didn't actually have to pass right by, but they made a detour to ride in the shadow of the stadium. Louie said a prayer, as he always did. "May we play here one day," he said, and Sally nodded.

"Mariano's retired, so they need a reliever," said Sally.

"Maybe you," said Louie.

They rode their bikes in the summer sun along the six-lane Grand Concourse, with their dogs on leashes trailing behind, to One Hundred Sixty-fifth Street and then onto Louie's street, Sheridan Avenue. They skidded their bikes to a stop on the sidewalk outside his house, a small two-story residence with a pointy roof and shutters on the windows.

"You staying for dinner?" Louie asked.

"What are you having?"

"Oh, brother," he said, shaking his head and going inside.

Chasing after him, Sally called out, "Sorry, sorry, it doesn't matter what you're having. Really, it doesn't."

What they were having that night, at the Cohen residence, was roasted chicken, mashed potatoes with gravy, asparagus with butter, green salad with big summer tomatoes, and warm, just-baked bread straight from the oven, all served in the dining room around an oval table.

"You're there, Sally, your usual seat," said Louie's father, Albert. Everyone called him Al. He was fifty, with thinning hair, a strong frame, and rough hands that had seen a construction site more than once. He tended to nod when you spoke, as if to make you feel better about what you were saying. He had deep-set brown eyes and a high forehead.

"Thanks, Mr. Cohen," Sally said. It was true she came to dinner maybe two or three times a week, maybe because her homelife wasn't so good. Louie never asked. She just came to dinner.

"Mimi, can we help?" yelled Al to his wife in the kitchen.

"No, I'm coming," yelled back Louie's mom.

A moment later, carrying the breadbasket in her lap, she wheeled herself into the dining room in her wheelchair right up to her seat at the table. Sally jumped up to help.

"It's all right, dear. I have it," said Mimi. She was a young mom, way too young to be in a wheelchair, but there she was—pretty, with straight brown hair, hazel eyes, soft features, strong arms from pushing the wheelchair, and a lean strong body, at least from the waist up. Her legs dangled off the wheelchair. Mimi pulled herself up to the end of the table, opposite Al. Sally sat back down and surveyed the heaping platters of chicken, potatoes, salad, and asparagus. It all smelled soooo good.

"Wow," said Sally, "my mother can't cook like this ever, and she's not in a—" She drew in a fast breath. "Sorry," she blurted out.

"It's all right, dear," said Mimi calmly. "I don't mind."

"I'm so sorry," Sally blathered on. "Really I am."

"Sally, it's okay. She knows she's in a wheelchair," said Louie. "Don't you, Mom?"

"Know it?" said Mimi breezily. "I've been in a wheelchair for seven years, so I ought to know it." She turned to the young girl. "But, Sally, I won't tell your mother you said that about her cooking."

"Noooooooooo," protested Sally, and everyone chuckled.

"Okay, phones away," ordered Mimi, and they slid their phones into their pockets; even Al hid his. "And dogs under the table." Louie lifted the tablecloth and Chester and Marmalade slid under.

"Who wants mashed potatoes?" said Al, passing them to Sally.

They piled their plates, ate, passed the platters, ate some more, and Louie went into the kitchen for more bread and came back, and they passed the platters and ate even more.

"It's so good," said Sally. "Thank you, Mrs. Cohen."

"You don't have to thank me, Sally," said Mimi. "You're part of the family."

"I heard you had a little trouble at the park today," said Al.

Louie put down his fork. "Just Froggy."

"Anything I can do?" asked his dad.

"Yeah, you can call his father and tell him what a jerk his son is," said Sally.

Both parents raised their eyebrows. "Or not," she said, shrugging.

"It's all right, Dad," said Louie. "We got this."

Chapter Two
A DOCTOR IN QUEENS

After dinner, Sally said goodbye and went home, and Louie climbed the stairs to his bedroom. It was painted *Yankee* colors, but you would hardly know it, because almost every inch of wall space was taken up with Yankees stuff: posters, Yankees jerseys, Yankees hats, photos of Dexter Archer and Mariano Rivera and all the new players, like Tom Lambert and Gavin Chavez. Even the ceiling was filled with hanging baseball bats, a giant photo of Yankee stadium (it took up almost the whole ceiling), and a giant NY Yankee logo decal. It was basically a Yankee paradise. On his shelf, each in a round little stand, were sixteen signed baseballs, all in a row. And the most prized possession, the one that held the place of honor, was a foul ball hit off the bat of Dexter Archer, which Louie had caught in his glove one magical night right before Archer hit a walk-off home run. And what a catch Louie made on the foul ball! It got him highlighted on ESPN that night. Louie! On ESPN!!!

Another ball was signed by Morgan and another by Arnold Rappoport, both of which Louie got signed by waiting by the clubhouse door till they came out after the game. Two of the other baseballs were signed by a machine, but Louie didn't care.

Stacked on his floor, between the desk and the bed, were hundreds of programs, a program for every game that Louie had ever gone to—from his first game at the age of four to the last game two weeks ago at the age of thirteen. Starting at about the age of eight, his dad had taught him how to keep score in the box score sheet, with pencil lines running horizontally for hits, diamond lines for bases, outs recorded, as well as hits, walks, errors. He wouldn't go to a game now without a pencil, an eraser that he rarely used anymore, and three bucks for a program.

In one corner of the room, Louie stacked his baseball equipment, his glove, his bat, and his baseballs—one that was ratty and totally beat up, one smudged with a little dirt, and one brand new—not to be used before the next game. It was the third year for his beat-up glove. He knew he should get a new one, but he loved his glove, and every time he speared a grounder or caught a line drive in the webbing, he knew he couldn't part with it. Not yet.

He switched on the radio (his parents wouldn't let him have a TV in his room) to catch the game, coming in from Cleveland. He heard the crowd noise first, so he knew the game was on, and then came the voice of the announcer:

"Lambert steps in, batting .294, for his first plate appearance tonight. He went three for four last night in Baltimore, with a double and three RBI's. Tonight he's going against Jaspers, and career he's only .197 against the right-hander, so he has his work cut out for him . . ."

Louie knew immediately he had missed the first two batters in the Yankee lineup—Morgan and Franklin—as Lambert batted third. But he'd had to say goodbye to Sally and have another piece of homemade blueberry pie his mother had made. And he knew he hadn't missed much, that the first two batters hadn't done much, because the play-by-play would be more exciting.

Lambert hit a fly ball to center for an out, to end the inning. Opening his backpack, Louie took out his homework, lined the books up carefully on his desk, turned on his laptop, and went to work on his homework—with one ear open, listening to the game.

It was later in the sixth inning, with the Yanks down 4–2, during the commercial break, that the radio went silent just for an instant. And in that moment, Louie heard talking downstairs. Talking downstairs wasn't all that uncommon. He heard his parents talking downstairs all the time, but something about this conversation was different; there was just something about it. So, Louie got up and went to the door, stuck his head out, and listened. But he couldn't make out what they were saying, so he slid out of his room and went quietly to the top of the stairs. Now he could make out his mother speaking to his father and his father, after a pause, saying something back. It sounded serious. He went down two stairs, then another two. He sat down and listened, just out of sight. Here on the lower stair, he could hear them clearly.

"It might not work," his mother was saying.

"We won't know till we talk to him," insisted his father.

"I just don't know if I want to go through all that," she said with a sigh.

"Listen, we go, we talk to him, and we see. There's no harm in that."

"There's no harm, I know, but . . ."

"But what?" said Al. "We just go."

"What if—"

Louie got up and walked down a few more stairs— to hear even better.

"We just go and talk to the doctor," his dad was saying.

Louie suddenly stood up, walked down the last few stairs, crossed the entry hall, and walked into the room. His mom and dad stopped talking as soon as they saw him come in and froze.

"What's going on?" asked Louie.

"Hello, dear," said his mother, putting on a smile.

"What?" persisted Louie. "What are you talking about?"

Mimi looked at Al, and he nodded. "Sit down, Louie," she said softly. So, Louie took a seat on the sofa.

"Louie, there's this doctor in Queens," started his father.

"Yeah?" said Louie.

"He's a neurosurgeon."

"A what?"

"A doctor who does surgery on the spine, a special doctor," said his mom.

"Oh. Okay."

"His name is Dr. Gupta, and . . ." Her words trailed off.

"And what?" Louie said.

"He wants to perform an operation on your mother…that might help," said his father.

"Help what?"

"Help her to walk again," said his dad.

"You might walk again?" Louie said loudly, jumping off the sofa.

"Now, don't get excited, not yet," said his father. "It's experimental. There's no guarantee that it will work—"

"You might *walk* again?"

"It's possible, but—" said Mimi.

"You might *walk again*?" said Louie.

"Yes. If it works," she said softly.

"Okay, then we're going to do it, right?" said Louie.

"Well . . ."

"Well, what?"

"We're going to the doctor tomorrow, so we'll see," said Al.

"You're going to the doctor tomorrow?"

"Yes," said his mom. "We have an appointment –"

"Can I go?" Louie cut in.

They didn't answer for a stunned moment, just looked at him, not knowing what to say. Mimi cleared her throat. "You want to go to the doctor with us?" she asked.

"I'm going," said Louie, settling the matter. "I'm going."

"Are you sure?" asked Mimi, her voice cracking.

"Gotta get back to the game," said Louie, heading back upstairs.

"Louie," called his mother after him, but Louie took the stairs three at a time and disappeared. Al looked at Mimi and shrugged.

"Why not?" he said.

"I'm not sure about all this," said Mimi, with some sadness creeping into her voice, and her hands holding the arms on the wheelchair. "I just don't know."

Chapter Three
THE SEEING EYE DOG

The Mount Sinai Hospital in Queens had no parking in front, so they had to drive around the block and find parking in a lot on Thirtieth Avenue. Al drove the family Ford pickup truck, the double cab, with Louie in the back seat and Mimi's wheelchair in the truck bed, strapped down alongside Chester, who sat straight up as if guarding the wheelchair. Al pulled into the parking space, and Louie jumped down to grab the wheelchair, pulling it out. Al lifted Mimi in his arms and placed her gently in it. Louie put his arm on it to keep it from moving back. Chester curled up in the back of the truck.

"Sorry, boy, no dogs allowed," said Louie. Chester wagged his tail to say he understood.

After passing through hospital corridor after corridor, the kind with shiny floors and bulletin boards on the walls, they went up an elevator, came out into a long hallway, wheeled past the cafeteria, went up in another elevator, came out on another corridor, and wheeled down the hallway to a room that was marked, NEUROLOGY. Louie wheeled his mother in. In a deserted waiting room with four rows of chairs, a woman sat behind scratched glass. Louie parked his mother over by the window to gaze out over Queens, while Al went up to the receptionist. Mimi didn't say much, just looked out. Al checked her in and then came back. And they waited.

"Mimi Cohen," called the receptionist, a half hour later.

They went through the door and down a hallway, into the doctor's office, with a large window and three office chairs. There was a poster on the wall with a diagram of the spine. Louie looked it over carefully. The spine curved one way and then another. It showed the vertebral column with nerves and muscles around the spinal column. He stared at it, trying to figure out how the back worked.

"Come sit down," said his mother.

He went over and sat down next to her and they looked out the window. You could see a lot from the fourth floor of the hospital. A nurse stuck her head in.

"Dr. Gupta will be right with you," she said and left. Mimi fidgeted with her wheelchair. A few moments later the door opened and a kindly-looking man came in, wearing a white coat, with a broad smile, bushy eyebrows, and wire-rimmed glasses.

"Hello," said Dr. Gupta.

He got right down to business. He opened his laptop and placed it on the desk, hit a few keys and brought up an image. "This is the MRI taken last time you were here, you remember?" He pointed to an MRI image of Mimi's spine.

"Yes, I remember," said Mimi.

"I've compared this image with the MRI taken right after the accident, years ago," he said, "and the good news is that it is not getting any worse."

"That's good," said Al.

"Yes, that's good," said Dr. Gupta. He pointed to the spine in several places. "In the accident, the spinal cord was severed here, and here, and here to some extent. You can see here that over time the vertebrae fused, and that gave you some stability but also cut off the blood flow to the spine."

"I see," said Mimi, her face darkening.

"And now this area of the spine here is inert," the doctor continued.

"Inert?" Louie asked. He had never heard that word.

"Not used," explained the doctor. "Under those circumstances, the nerve roots become blocked and fail, making it impossible to stand or walk."

"And now, what would we do, if we had this operation?" asked Al.

"Ah, yes, I knew you would ask," said the doctor, with a quick smile. "Well, it's new, a very new operation, but we would reattach the nerves here, here, and here"—his stubby index finger pointing to the spine in three places—"and then put peristaltic rods here to reconnect the bony matter and the nerves."

"That's a lot, Doctor. Could you—"

"Yes, of course." The kind doctor took a breath. "By stabilizing the spine, we let the nerves reattach over time, and with stability she just might—"

"Walk again?" Louie blurted out.

"Perhaps," said the doctor.

"She *might* walk again, or she *will*?"

"It's experimental. That's all I can tell you," said Dr. Gupta. "But it's possible."

"And who would do the operation?" asked Mimi.

"I would, here in the hospital. It's a long operation, so I would have two doctors assisting me."

"How long?" asked Al.

"Six, maybe seven hours, if all goes well," said Dr. Gupta.

"That long?" Mimi looked skeptical.

"Maybe longer. It's a big operation."

"Well, it's something to think about," said Al.

Dr. Gupta rose. "There's no hurry. Talk it over and—"

"She's doing it," said Louie abruptly.

"Louie," cautioned his mother.

"She's going to have the operation," said Louie. "It's decided."

Dr. Gupta looked Louie over, and a smile came across his face. "You're a Yankees fan?" he asked.

"Yes."

"So am I."

"Who's your favorite player?" asked Louie. It was a question he always asked right away to see if people really were Yankees fans.

"Of all time or on the roster today?" replied Dr. Gupta calmly. Good response, thought Louie.

"All time."

"That's easy. Mariano." Louie sized him up. He noticed that he had keys hanging from his belt and his keychain had a little Yankees souvenir bat. So, he really was a Yankees fan.

"Doctor, we'll have to talk this over," said Al.

"Of course, of course." The door opened, and a woman came in, wearing a nice salmon-colored jacket with "Mt. Sinai" embroidered on it. "This is Ms. Monroe from administration, and she'll go over the details with you."

"Thank you, Doctor," said Al.

"Good luck with your decision," he said, slipping out.

Ms. Monroe, looking very efficient and businesslike, opened a file and sat down in the same chair where Dr. Gupta had been sitting. She wasn't as friendly, being all business, but her hair had been cut stylishly and her face was not unkind. She had well-manicured fingernails with pink polish, and smooth hands that moved quickly over the keyboard.

"Well, let's see," she said, bringing up the file. "I've been in touch with the insurance company." She looked up right at them.

"And?" said Al.

"I'm afraid I don't have good news."

"Why not?" said Louie.

"The insurance company has classified this operation as experimental."

"Experimental?" asked Al. "What does that mean?"

"They don't want to cover it."

"Not at all?" asked Mimi.

"They're putting up a fight," said Ms. Monroe. "I tried several times."

"And?"

"I'm afraid they've declined to cover the operation," said Ms. Monroe.

"What does that mean?" asked Louie.

"It means the insurance company won't pay," said Al sharply.

"Why not?"

"They don't always pay, dear," said Mimi gently.

Louie turned to Ms. Monroe. "How much is it?" he asked. "How much would the operation cost?"

"Well, let's see." Ms. Monroe looked over the file. "There's the pre-op that would be done here—then the surgery, here also, and the recovery at the rehab center.

You'd be in the hospital for about two weeks, and there's physical therapy afterwards. Dr. Gupta has reduced his surgeon fee to help some, but that's only a small part of the overall charge."

"And just how much is the overall charge?" asked Al. "The whole thing—out the door."

"Seven hundred and fifty," said Ms. Monroe, looking down.

"Seven hundred and fifty . . . what?" asked Mimi.

"Thousand," she said.

"What?!!" gasped Mimi.

Al blinked several times. "Seven hundred and fifty thousand *dollars*?" he asked.

"Yes, I'm afraid so. Seven hundred and fifty thousand dollars," she repeated.

"Well, that's the end of that," said Mimi. "Let's go."

"I'm sorry," said Ms. Monroe. "I tried."

"Won't insurance pay anything?" Al persisted.

"No," she said, "they declined us."

"Can you still have the operation?" asked Louie. It was all going so fast, he didn't get it.

"We'll talk about it at home," said his mother.

The end of the visit went by in a blur. Louie wheeled his mother out. They went back down the long corridors with the shiny floors, into the elevator, down another hall, into another elevator, and out to the parking lot. Chester sat up to greet them. Al picked Mimi up and carried her to the passenger seat, and

Louie folded up the wheelchair and strapped it in the truck bed next to Chester. No one said much. Al backed the truck up and drove out of the lot, stopping to pay the parking fee at the booth. They came out on Thirtieth Avenue.

"Louie, look," said Al. Louie looked over. A black Labrador seeing-eye dog was guiding a blind woman across the street. The dog stopped at the light, checking for cars this way and that, and then, when the light changed, took the woman through the crosswalk, slowing down so she would know the curb was coming, and helped her step up and walk towards the front door of the hospital.

"You could do that, couldn't you, boy?" said Louie through the back window to Chester, who got up and wagged his tail. They drove on and Louie looked out the window.

"He's a Yankees fan," said Louie, calmly, after a while.

"Who?" said Mimi.

"The doctor."

They drove home, to their small house with the pointy roof on Sheridan Avenue in the Bronx. Al carried Mimi inside, and grabbing his glove, Louie ran off to the park with Chester for baseball practice. But he didn't play well, going 0 for 4, with two strikeouts, mostly because he was thinking about the hospital and the doctor who was a Yankees fan—and the operation his mother was definitely going to have, because he was going to find the money, one way or another. Of that, he was sure.

Chapter Four
FINDING A WAY

That night, after dinner, Louie and his father cleared everything off the dining room table, spread out all the statements from the bank and retirement accounts, and popped open the laptop. Chester curled up under the table, and Mimi came in and sat down across from them, stone-faced, crossing her arms. She didn't like what was going on, and she wanted them to know. They paid no attention.

"Okay, I think I got this figured out," said Al, plucking the keys and entering numbers into his spreadsheet.

"What is it?" asked Louie.

"We have about fifty thousand dollars in our 401K."

"That's our retirement money," Mimi protested. They looked up at her, then back at the statements.

"There'll be a small penalty to take it out, but we'll get a tax break on the medical expenses."

"So that's fifty," said Louie.

"Right."

"Then what?"

"Well, I spoke with the mortgage company today and we can ref-fi the house and come away with about seventy-five."

"Seventy-five thousand?" asked Louie.

"Yeah, so that's seventy-five and fifty, so that gives us one hundred twenty-five thousand dollars."

"Al," said Mimi sternly. Al looked at her, then went back to his laptop.

"And I spoke with the bank today, and they said we qualified for a personal loan of about thirty-five thousand," he said.

"No," repeated Mimi, rolling her wheelchair up closer to the table. "I said, no."

"So," asked Louie, "how much does that give us all together?"

Al crunched the numbers. He typed in "$50,000" and under that "$75,000" and under that "$35,000." He hit total.

"That's one hundred and sixty thousand dollars," he said.

"And how much do we need?"

"We need seven hundred and fifty thousand dollars."

"What about my account?" asked Louie.

"Your college savings?" demanded Mimi. "No. Absolutely not."

Al pulled out the bank statement and held it up.

"You've got about sixty thousand dollars in there."

"That's his college money!" Mimi said harshly.

"So, with that, how much do we have?" Louie asked his father.

"If we took it all," he said, with a sidelong glance at Mimi, "we'd have two hundred and twenty thousand dollars."

"How much do we need, again?"

"Seven hundred and fifty."

"So, what do we still need?"

Al tallied it up. "We need five hundred and thirty thousand dollars."

"More?" asked Louie, the word catching in his throat.

"More," Al confirmed.

"We are not going to be ruined financially," Mimi said. "We're not."

"Mom."

"I'll be fine. I'll just stay in this wheelchair."

"No!" yelled Louie, jumping up. "We'll get the money. We'll get it."

"But Louie, we can't—"

"I said, we'll get it—and we'll get it," Louie yelled. Chester looked up at Louie, who pushed back his chair and ran out of the dining room. By the time Louie had run up his stairs and got to his room, Chester was by his side. They went in together, and Louie shut the door.

Louie fell face down on the bed. Chester came over and put his nose next to Louie's face.

"It's okay, boy," said Louie, turning to him. "We'll get it."

Chester went over to the radio on the desk and hit the ON button with his nose, and that familiar crowd noise at the baseball park filled the room.

"Garner lays off the fastball high and inside . . . the infield is in, hoping to get a play at the plate . . . Garner steps back in . . . and Calloway delivers. Ball low and inside. Garner steps out and gets the sign from third . . ."

A light tapping on his door.

"What?" said Louie. His dad came in.

Al sat down at the end of the bed. "What your mother is saying," he said, "is that it's a lot of money, and money doesn't grow on trees—"

"Dad."

"Yes, son?"

"We'll get it."

"But, Louie, we don't want you thinking that we can—"

"Dad."

"Yes?"

"We'll find the money."

Smiling, Al gave Chester a pat. "Chester, do you happen to have five hundred and thirty thousand dollars on you? No, you don't, do you? But if you did, you'd give it to us, wouldn't you?" Chester barked.

His father got up and started out, stopping to look at the giant wall poster of Dexter Archer. "What do you think Dexter Archer's doing these days, now that he's retired?" he asked. Louie rolled over without saying anything, so Al gave Chester a last pat and quietly left the room.

"Garner hits a ground ball into the hole, and that will score Martinez from third . . ."

Chapter Five
MAKING LEMONADE

They passed a sign that read COHEN CONSTRUCTION on their way in. Al pulled up to the worksite in his pickup truck—with Louie in the passenger seat and Chester in the back. It was a hot June morning. In the summer, with school out, Louie often went with his dad to the construction site and helped the guys. Being thirteen, he was too young to have an actual job, but his dad said it was okay and brought him along. He got paid ten dollars an hour, cash, at the end of the day. Al owned Cohen Construction, Inc., which built office buildings in the boroughs of Queens and the Bronx, usually five-or ten-story jobs, with nice lobbies and nice offices, and lots of windows. The project today, in Bayside, was a new building to house a health club, a smoothie bar, a barbershop, a hair salon, and a candle store, with some apartments above the stores. It was early in the construction, in the concrete and rebar phase, and when they arrived, the guys were hoisting a large piece of concrete with a crane, guiding it into place.

"Okay, let's go," said Al. Louie got out. And Chester jumped down, looking like he owned the place. The workers waved and yelled, "Hiya, Chester."

"I got my A-team today," Al yelled back to his guys. "Louie and Chester."

Louie went to work with the pipefitter, Griego. Griego had worked with Louie, so he was aware that Louie knew what he was doing, after so many days on the job, so he let him turn the wrench and even call out the measurements for the pipe cutter. "You always get it right," said Griego.

"One-inch pipe, boy," yelled Louie, and Chester ran to the rack, pulled out a one-inch pipe ten feet long, and dragged it back.

"He good boy, too," said Griego. "Good Chester."

They took a coffee break at ten, with Al pouring Louie a touch of coffee with lots of milk so he could be one of the guys. Al brought some architectural plans for the second floor, spread them out, and they all gathered around to look them over.

"The rebar has to go here, here, and over here," said Al. "I'll mark it." He patted his front pocket for something to write with but had nothing. "Somebody got a pencil?" he asked. They heard a dog whine from above and looked up and saw Chester standing on a girder, with a pencil in his mouth. He dropped it right into Al's hand. "Chester," he said, shaking his head, "get down from there." Chester hopped down.

"After lunch, we'll drop in the concrete blocks," Al said. Lunch was a salami-and-cheese sandwich made by his mother. She made it big, knowing it was one bite for Louie, one bite for Chester, until it was gone. The workers threw scraps to Chester too—a bit of a burrito, a bit of stew, a bit of roast beef—so he had plenty. "He's a working dog," said Griego.

"Okay, back to work," called out Al, closing up his lunchbox.

The guys knew how to guide the large concrete blocks into place and secure them. It could be dangerous; the crane operator had to be precise. The crane operator had to keep the concrete from swaying too much and hitting something. He started up the crane with a roar and tightened the cable on a big piece of concrete for the interior wall. The guys wrapped the cable securely around the block, stepped back, and gave the signal to the crane operator, who hauled it up in the air and swung it across the worksite. Al held up his arm to guide it as it moved into place. At his signal, the operator slowed the crane as it came into position.

"Down," Al called out. The operator hit the down lever, letting the cable out and lowering the concrete block, which slowly dropped towards the outstretched arms of Al and three of his men.

"Okay, keep it coming," yelled Al. "Okay, hold . . . Okay, down. Hold . . . Okay, down... hold." He grabbed the cable above the block, yanking it, and the other guys grabbed the side of the block, maneuvering it into the slot prepared ahead of time. "More," yelled Al. The operator gently let out the cable and the concrete dropped perfectly into place with a clunk. Two of the guys wrapped it with giant straps to secure it. "Okay, who's got the level?" Al yelled, and when he looked down, there was Chester already standing there, holding the level in his mouth.

"Thanks, boy," he said, taking the level and checking the concrete block. "Tie it down," he yelled, and the guys moved to secure it permanently. "Chester gets hazard pay," said Al, and the guys laughed. Chester wagged his tail.

When the workday ended, and the guys were cleaning up the site, Al walked over to Louie and handed him four twenty-dollar bills. Louie took out a small notebook and wrote down "$80" in it.

"I'll bet I know where that's going," said his dad.

"Only five hundred twenty-nine thousand, nine hundred and twenty bucks to go," said Louie, and they both laughed.

When they got home about three o'clock, Sally was waiting outside with her bat and glove. Louie jumped out. "I can't play today," he said to her.

"Why not?" said Sally.

"Yeah, why not?" asked his father.

"Just can't," he said. "Come on, boy." They ran down the block.

"Where you going?" yelled his father.

"Be right back."

Al looked at Sally and shrugged and he and Sally watched Louie disappear around the corner. Louie ran down Nineteenth Avenue, crossed Bayside, and entered the corner market. From the produce section he picked out a dozen large lemons. He picked up two pounds of sugar and bought a large plastic pitcher with the ounce lines on the side. He bought a rawhide for Chester, paid for it with the cash he just got from the jobsite, handed the rawhide to Chester, and ran back home, with Chester close behind. Sally was still there, staring at him as if he'd gone bonkers.

Louie went inside to the kitchen, where his mother was moving around in her wheelchair, starting dinner, and he took out a knife and cut each lemon in half.

"What are you doing?" she asked.

"Making lemonade," he said.

"To take to the field?"

"No," he said, but that's all he said.

He put the fresh lemon juice in the pitcher and filled it with water from the sink; then he took out a large spoon, poured in the sugar, and stirred. He went to the cupboard and took out the paper cups Mom always kept there.

"What do you need those for?" asked Mimi.

"Just do," said Louie.

He ran out of the kitchen, down to the garage, found the folding table and brought it out to the street. He got the large piece of cardboard from the garage, wrote LEMONADE $2 on it, and taped it to the front of the table. Then he set up the cups and the pitcher.

"You're selling lemonade?" asked Sally.

"Yeah," said Louie.

"Why?"

He didn't answer. He looked up the street and saw no one. He looked the other way and saw no one. A car drove by and didn't stop.

"I'll buy one," said Sally, stepping up.

"No."

"Why not? I'm thirsty."

"Only paying customers."

"I'll pay."

"Forget it," he said, and poured her a glass and handed it to her. She took out two dollars. "No," he said.

A car slowed and stopped, and a woman rolled down her window. Louie didn't wait for her to order, just poured her one and took it to the car. "Two dollars," he said. She handed him two dollars and drove off.

When Louie got back to his table, two kids were waiting, and he sold two more. "That's six bucks," said Sally. "You're rich."

In the house, Mimi wheeled her wheelchair over to the window. Al came up next to her and they watched together, looking down as Louie put the money in his cash bucket.

"This isn't right," said Mimi. "He should be at the park."

"You never know," said Al wryly, "he might sell a lot of lemonade."

Mimi wiped a tear away with her hand. "I never should have started this," she said.

"I'll go talk to him," said Al, heading out.

"Two dollars, please," said Louie to a customer as he raked in another sale. Al walked up and looked over the operation.

"Hi, Mr. Cohen," said Sally. She motioned with her head towards Louie, as if to say, *what's with him?*

"Hi, Sally."

"Louie's selling lemonade," she said.

"I can see that," said Al.

"I got twelve bucks already," said Louie.

"Isn't it time for baseball practice?" asked his dad. Louie didn't answer but bit his lower lip. "Louie, why don't you let me take over while you go play?" Louie hesitated, unsure. "I've sold a lot of lemonade in my day," reassured his father.

"Okay, the extra lemonade is under the table, the cups are there, and the money goes into that bucket," said Louie breathlessly.

"Got it."

"Thanks, Dad."

"Okay, you take off. I got this."

Louie ran inside, grabbed his glove and bat, flew back out the front door, and he and Sally raced towards the park, with Chester and Marmalade galloping alongside. An elderly man walked up and ordered a lemonade.

"That'll be two dollars," said Al.

Chapter Six
TOUCHING THIRD BASE

A frisbee spun by. It flew for twenty, thirty, forty, fifty yards, half the length of a football field over the grass, and Oscar the German Shepherd, hot on the chase, got under it, pushed off, made a spectacular leap and caught it. In another part of the park, Pearl the Scotty chased fly balls off Donna's bat. Champ the Collie barked every time the batter swung at the ball as it crossed the plate. Cocking her ears in a funny way whenever Sally threw a curveball, Marmalade stood behind her on the pitcher's mound. And Chester was behind first base, watching—and barking when somebody made a good play. It was a practice day for the Bronx Badgers.

"Curveball," said Sally from the mound, winding up and pitching. Marmalade watched it go over the plate. She cocked her ears. "Steeee-riiiiike," said Sally. "Did you see that, Marmy?"

"Okay, bring it in," yelled Louie. The kids and their dogs came running in and gathered around.

"Ron, did Bernie get his medicine?"

"Yep, and he's not throwing up anymore."

"Now, that's something we should all be happy about," Sally said.

"Cara, how's Donut's leg?"

"Much better. Look." Cara put her fingers to her mouth and whistled. Donut the Mutt came running, her little legs spinning at full speed, and she slid in at Cara's feet.

"Sign her," said Sally. "She's got talent."

"And Veronica, how's Gabby's cut?"

"All healed up," responded Veronica. She threw a ball up high, Gabby ran hard, got under it, and caught it.

"Okay," said Sally. "Let's pick."

That meant a pickup game, and they divided up for a three-inning practice game. Juan was captain of one team and Donna the other. Louie and Sally ended up on the same team, Louie at third base and Sally on the mound.

"Dogs in the dug," yelled Louie. And the kids rounded them up and put them in the dugout in a sit-stay.

The first pitch Sally threw was hit for a line drive double to right-center field.

"There goes the perfect game," said Sally, wryly. "Can't always be perfect."

"I thought you were," said Louie.

"Yeah, well, there's that." Sally then struck out the next two batters, and Louie speared a hard ground ball hit down the line and threw out the runner at first for the final out of the inning, stranding the runner on second. When they came up, Sally bunted her way to first in the bottom of the inning, stole second, and Louie drove her home with a single to right.

It was in the top of the third inning, with two outs, when Levar came up. He hit a weird little spin ball that rolled between the pitcher's mound and first base and got through for an infield single. Cara, up next, hit a hard grounder into the hole between second and third, and it looked like it would get through. But Chip knocked it down to hold the runner at second. Runners were now on first and second, and Juan came up to bat. Juan took the first pitch, a strike. He crowded the plate, looking for an inside pitch. Sally pitched him outside and he let it go by. A ball.

Juan stepped out and looked over the field. Louie was playing off the base at third. Juan stepped back in. Sally delivered—a fastball on the inside corner. Juan turned on it and ripped a low liner down the left field line, a screamer. Louie dove for it but missed it by inches. The ball zipped past him and headed for left field. But Chester saw it. He was standing in foul territory, just off the line. Seeing the ball zip under Louie's glove, he lunged and caught it in his mouth a few yards behind third base and lifted his head, holding the ball. Louie looked up from the grass and saw Chester standing there with the ball in his mouth.

"Third," yelled Louie. "Touch the base!"

Chester's ears pricked up and he looked befuddled. Levar was running hard for third, dirt flying.

"Touch third, boy," yelled Louie, pointing to third base. "Touch third."

In that moment, Chester got it. He pushed off his back legs and bolted towards the base. Levar slid. Chester lunged—and touched the base just ahead of the runner, the ball still firmly in his mouth.

"Out," shouted Sally, running over. "You're out."

"No way," shouted Levar back. "I can't be."

"Out," yelled Sally. "I saw it."

"You can't be out by a *dog*," Levar bellowed.

"He touched it first," said Sally. "You're out."

"You're all out!" said a voice. They all stopped and looked up. There was Froggy and his team standing there, holding their bats and gloves. Louie got up off the dirt. Sally walked in. The whole team gathered around.

"What are you doing here?" asked Louie.

"Have you come to learn more numbers?" asked Sally. "We can work on getting to twenty."

"Very funny."

"We told you, it's our field," said Louie.

"Yeah, I know, but . . ." said Froggy—and how he said it, calmly and confidently, bothered Louie.

"But what?" said Sally.

"Well," said Froggy. "You forgot one thing."

"What?"

"I'll show ya." Froggy walked over to the backstop, grabbed onto the chain link fence, and climbed up until he reached the sign that said: DOGS ALLOWED.

"What do we have here?" Froggy said.

"Uh-oh," said Sally quietly to Louie.

Louie bit his lip. Froggy peeled off one strip of tape. "Why, what's this?" He pulled off another strip of tape, then another, then another, until the NO was visible again. And now the sign read: NO DOGS ALLOWED.

"That's funny, Froggy," said Sally. "I didn't think you could read."

Froggy climbed back down. "Now, take your dogs and get off," he said.

"They're not hurting anyone," said Louie.

"We're not getting off, Froggy. We don't care what you say," said Sally.

"Well, that could be a problem." Froggy took out his cell phone and started to dial.

"What are you doing?" demanded Sally. Froggy kept dialing. "Froggy, what are you doing?"

"Hello, is this Animal Control?" Froggy said into the phone.

"Froggy, stop," demanded Sally.

"Hi, I'd like to report a gang of wild dogs on the loose."

"Froggy!" said Sally.

"Yes," said Froggy, "wild, vicious dogs roaming the park."

"Froggy, please don't—" said Sally, hoping that might work.

"Where? You can find them at—"

"All right," said Louie.

"Hold on a minute," Froggy said, covering the phone with his hand. "All right what?"

"We'll get off."

"You'll get off?"

"I said we would, and we will," said Louie angrily.

"Louie," said Sally.

"The dogs," he said.

"Sorry, wrong number," Froggy said into the phone, and hung up. "Okay, we're on," he yelled to his team. "We got the field."

"You're a jerk, Froggy," said Sally.

"I may be a jerk," he replied, "but I'm a jerk with a field."

"Okay, let's go," Louie called to his team. He and Chip and Juan and Cara and Ron and Chuck and Levar and Veronica and Donna and Sally all gathered up their stuff, slowly, leashed their dogs, Pal and Oscar and Donut and Bernie and Bull and Champ and Gabby and Pearl and Marmalade and Chester—and slowly, inching along, started to move, heads down.

"We got a game to play here," Froggy yelled, "so move it."

Sally wheeled on them. "Froggy, *these dogs* can play baseball better than you."

Froggy and his teammates cracked up. "Well, when they can play, come on back and we'll play 'em," said Froggy, doubling over.

Sally looked like she might have a fit, but before she could lay a right hook on him, Louie broke in. "Come on," he said. And he led his team off the field. They trudged past Mr. Park's market.

"You no play today?" said Mr. Park, his eyebrows furrowing, picking up his broom.

"Not today," said Sally.

"No baseball?"

"Not today," said Louie.

They moved on towards home. And Chester didn't bark, not today.

Chapter Seven
THEY CAN PLAY!

"Don't worry, we'll find another field," said Sally, as they walked along Grand Concourse Avenue past the shops, past the bikes tied up to the parking meters, past the bakery.

"No, we won't," Louie replied harshly. "This is New York City. Just where do you think we're going to find another baseball field?"

"I don't know," she said. "I never had to think about it before."

It was a really hot day, and some kids had found a wrench and opened a fire hydrant on Grand Concourse Avenue. It was blasting water all over the sidewalk, and the screaming kids were running through the spray before the cops got there and shut it down. Normally, Louie would have been all over that, but today he just walked on by, even as Sally dunked her head in the water to cool off.

"Don't want to?" she asked, catching up to him.

"No."

They arrived outside his house.

"I should go home," she said.

"Just come in," he said sullenly, disappearing into the house.

His mother took one look at Louie and asked, "What's wrong?"

"Nothing." he said glumly.

"Not nothing," explained Sally. "We got kicked off the field."

"Well, tell me all about it," Mimi said. Sitting them down with some raspberry iced tea, she listened to Sally rattle on about how Froggy and his team threatened to call Animal Control on the dogs and have them taken away for being on the field illegally. When Al came in, she started over and told it all again.

"I'm going to my room," said Louie, and he ran up the stairs with Chester by his side. He threw himself on his bed, and Chester curled up next to him. He thought about all the dogs, Chester and Marmalade and Gabby and Bernie and Bull and all the rest of them, and how unfair it was—how they might never be able to go to the park again to watch them play baseball. A light tapping at his door.

"Your mother said to tell you it's dinner," said Sally softly. "Are you going to eat?"

Downstairs, Louie took his seat at the usual place, and Sally sat in her usual seat. Al sat at one head and wheeling her chair to the other head was Mimi. Only the sound of the wheelchair was heard on the floor. They passed the platters and ate quietly, the only sound being the scraping of the silverware on the plates.

"Well, one thing we know. You can't give up playing baseball," said Al, breaking the ice.

"I know, Dad," Louie said angrily.

"Could you go play without the dogs?" suggested his mother.

"Without Chester?" Louie yelled. "Without Marmalade? Or Pal or Donut or Pearl? We can't do that to them."

"I know," said Mimi softly, to soothe him. "I understand. It's just that life sometimes doesn't work out the way you want it to."

"The question is, what can be done?" Al said.

"We could go kick the crap out of them," said Sally. And they all stopped and looked at her. "Or not," she said.

"Well, there must be something," said Mimi.

"There isn't," said Louie, getting up from the table and storming out. A moment later the back door squeaked open and slammed shut.

"Let him go," said his mother. "He'll be all right."

Sally wasn't sure. She'd never seen Louie like this in all the years she'd known him. Louie always figured things out, came up with ideas, never got mad or let anything like this get to him. But not tonight.

The three of them—without Louie—finished dinner quietly, barely speaking. After the main course, Sally asked to be excused and Mimi said, "Of course, dear." Sally left the room. She went through the kitchen, through the back door, and out into the backyard. For a New York City house, even in the Bronx, the backyard was big, with an old elm tree in the right corner and an old rope swing. Louie had set up a small baseball diamond with a net to catch the foul balls so they didn't go over the fence. But now Louie wasn't playing baseball, or swinging a bat, or any of the other things he usually did. He was just sitting there.

That's where Sally found him, in the corner behind the tree, looking out with a somber face, biting his lower lip. Sally didn't know what to say, so she just sat down next to him. Chester went and dug up an old baseball and dropped it at Louie's feet. But Louie didn't move.

"He wants you to throw it," said Sally.

"I know," he shot back.

"Are you gonna?"

"Not now," said Louie.

Chester got down in a crouch, waiting for him to throw it, and looked up at Louie, then back at the ball.

"I said, not now," Louie said harshly.

Chester looked up at him with his big white face and black nose and cocked his head. He'd done this a thousand times, a million times, and Louie always threw it to him.

"Oh, I'll do it," said Sally. She picked up the baseball and threw it. Chester tore after it, speared it, made a fast turn and headed back.

"Good grab," said Sally. She turned back to Louie. He didn't even look up.

Chester brought the ball back and rolled it again to Louie's feet, but Louie just kicked it away.

"Stop it, Chester," he said roughly. "I said no."

"He just wants you to throw it," Sally said gently.

"Dogs can't play baseball," said Louie.

"Oh, yeah, watch this." Sally picked up the ball and threw a high fly. Chester ran under it and caught it near the fence. He came back running at full speed and threw himself into a slide on his tummy and dropped the ball at Louie's feet.

"Stop it, Chester," yelled Louie, kicking the ball away.

"What's the matter with you?" said Sally. "I've never seen you yell at Chester before."

"Well, why not?" he replied sullenly. "We just got kicked off our field and we're stuck in this backyard."

"It's not Chester's fault. He just wants to play baseball," she said.

Sally picked up the bat, tossed up the ball, and hit a grounder. In spite of himself, Louie looked up. He saw Chester spear the grounder and run it back. And while he watched Chester bring back the ball, Louie remembered seeing Oscar catch the frisbee. He remembered watching the seeing-eye dog lead that woman across the street at the hospital. And he thought back to Chester touching third base to make the out on Levar.

"Huh," he muttered, mostly to himself, but Sally heard it.

"Huh, what?"

"Huh."

Louie got up, took the ball, and threw a high fly. Chester caught it. He grabbed his bat and hit a grounder. Chester grabbed it up and ran it in.

"Huh," said Louie.

"Huh what?" she said. "Stop saying that."

"I was just thinking…"

"About what?" asked Sally.

"I was wondering…"

"Louie, you're driving me nuts. What are you talking about?"

"What did Froggy say? When the dogs can play baseball, come on back and we'll play 'em. Right? Isn't that what he said?"

"Yeah? So?"

"Well, maybe they could…"

Mimi and Al were finishing the dishes and wrapping the leftovers when they heard Louie yelling from the backyard.

"Mom, Dad, come quick."

Exchanging a worried look, Al grabbed the wheel-chair and wheeled it out the back door onto the porch.

"What is it, dear?" asked Mimi, in her worried voice.

"They can play," said Louie.

"Who can play?" asked his father.

"The dogs," shouted Louie. "The dogs can play baseball."

"Can they?" said his mother, "Really?"

Mimi and Al nodded at their son with fake smiles plastered on their faces, like *uh-oh, it's okay, just humor the poor boy, our son has lost his marbles, and maybe, just maybe, we have a nutcase in the family.*

"That's nice, dear," said his mother. "Would anyone like some lemonade?"

Chapter Eight
FLING BALL

"I know it sounds crazy," pleaded Louie.

It was the next day and they were in the park. They just stared at him, like, *are you okay?* No one spoke. The whole team was there—Chip, Juan, Cara, Ron, Chuck, Levar, Veronica, and Donna—standing in a circle around Sally and Louie, with their chins hanging low and their mouths hanging open.

"No, it doesn't sound crazy," said Chuck finally, holding Bull the Bulldog by his leash. "Dogs playing baseball, sounds about right to me."

"Sure," said Donna. "Dogs playing baseball. Right. Everyone knows they can do that."

"I know it sounds crazy, but—" Louie said.

"I think the Yankees have some on their team," said Cara. "Don't they?"

"Oh, yeah," said Juan. "Don't they have a Terrier playing second base?"

"Yes," said Levar. "And they have a Collie playing center."

"Okay, okay," said Louie.

"I hear they have a Pug hitting cleanup," said Ron.

"Sure, everyone knows dogs can play baseball," said Cara.

"And they can do algebra."

"And take out the garbage."

"I have to wash the car this afternoon," said Veronica. "Maybe they could do that, too."

"I know it sounds crazy—" said Louie.

"Oh no," they all replied at once. "It doesn't sound crazy at all."

Louie put up his hand. "Just listen," he said. They all stopped and looked at him blankly. He took a deep breath. "Can dogs catch a frisbee at fifty yards?"

"Yeah," they all agreed, nodding.

"So, they can catch, just like we do?"

They nodded—grudgingly, but they nodded.

"Can they run?"

"Sure," they all said. "We'll give you that—all dogs can run."

"Can dogs be seeing-eye dogs?"

"Yeah . . ."

"So, they can learn when to cross the street?" continued Louie.

"Sure . . . guess so."

"Can dog learn to do tricks, like roll over and play dead?"

"Yeah . . ."

"So, dogs can catch, run, field, learn rules, and learn tricks. So then, why can't dogs learn to play baseball?"

After a pause, Veronica said, "Louie, are you on some new meds we need to know about?" The other kids nodded, like *yeah, that would make a lot of sense.*

"Louie," said Donna, "it's just not possible."

Sally stepped in. "Show them," she said.

"Show them?" said Louie.

"Yeah, just show them."

Louie brightened. "Okay," he said. "Let's run the bases." He put everyone out in the field, tossed the ball up and hit a line drive. Marmalade started running. She rounded first and headed for second. The throw came in from the outfield. Marmalade slid. And beat the tag.

"See?" said Louie. "Dogs can run the bases."

"How'd you get her to do that?" inquired Veronica.

"Look, maybe a dog can run around the bases, but it doesn't mean they can play baseball," said Donna.

"Okay, watch this." Louie hit a ground ball to Chester at short and took off for first. Chester knocked it down with his chest, scooped it up and ran for first, beating Louie by a step.

"But, Louie," said Chip. "Just because a dog can catch a ball doesn't mean they can *play baseball.*"

"Okay, how about this?"

Louie hit a grounder to Oscar, who stepped on second for the force out and ran to first ahead of the runner.

"There it is, a double play," said Sally. "By a bunch of dogs."

"Wow," said Juan.

"Amazing," said Chuck.

"Incredible," said Donna.

"Unbelievable," said Levar.

"Whatever," said Cara.

"Well, maybe dogs really can play baseball," said Veronica. "Who knew?"

Practice for the dogs started the next day. Though Van Cortland Park was huge, a thousand acres, there were no other baseball diamonds, only a big lawn, so they made their own baseball field, putting shirts down for bases and a used pizza box for home plate. The kids got their dogs into position in the field: Chester at first, Pearl the Scotty at second, Bernie the Bernese Mountain Dog at catcher, Bull the Bulldog at third, and the others in the outfield.

"Ready?" said Louie.

"Ready," said Sally, nodding her head.

"Okay, let's try this."

Louie hit a soft grounder to Bull the Bulldog at third base. Bull raced towards it, and it looked like he was going to field it perfectly. But then he stopped and watched it go through his legs into left field.

"Good start," said Sally.

"Let's try again," said Louie.

He hit a popup to Pearl the Scotty at second. She let it drop to the ground, then curled up and put her head down on the ball.

"Hmmm," said Sally. "Promising."

Louie then hit a fly ball to center field, and all the dogs took off after it, creating a massive clump of dogs in the outfield and no dogs in the infield.

"Nooooooo," wailed Louie. "Don't bunch up!"

"This may be harder than we thought," said Sally.

The dogs, with some prodding, got back to their positions. Louie hit a light grounder to third, and Bull the Bulldog caught it. "Good boy," yelled Louie. Then Bull, spotting a car driving by, took off after it with the ball in his mouth. "Maybe this wasn't such a good idea," said Louie.

"Don't give up yet," said Sally. "Try this."

Sally put Gabby the Bassett Hound at home plate and hit a fly ball. "Run, girl, run to first," she yelled. But Gabby ran the wrong way, up the line towards third base.

"Oh, brother," Louie sighed.

Mr. Park showed up with snacks—potato chips and oranges and cashews he brought over from the market.

"Dogs play baseball," he said, with that sly look he had. "Very funny. Dogs play baseball." And he went back to the market, chuckling all the way.

"Well, it was a good idea while it lasted," said Louie.

"Wait a minute, I got an idea," said Sally, looking over the snacks and dog treats Mr. Park brought.

"What?"

Sally pulled out the bag full of dog treats. "Watch this." She threw the ball to Pearl. When she caught it, she gave her a treat. After that Pearl caught the ball every time Sally threw it to her, getting a treat each time.

"Hm," said Louie. "Okay."

When Bull slid into second to break up the double play, Sally threw him a treat. After that, Bull broke up every double play.

When Louie hit a fly ball to center and Pal the Great Dane caught it, Sally threw him a leftover peanut butter sandwich.

"Easy," said Sally. "Food."

The kids gathered around.

"But Louie, but Louie," they all said at once.

"They can't throw—" said Donna.

"And if they can't throw, they can't play," said Ron.

"Right," said Louie, "I hadn't thought about that."

Wracking his brain on the way home that afternoon, Louie couldn't come up with anything. Dogs had to learn to throw or they couldn't play baseball. He knew that. But he didn't have any idea of what might work. So, that night in his garage, he and Sally got together and tried to get Chester to throw the ball. The Labrador could flip it with his mouth, but only a few feet.

"This is stupid," said Louie. "Maybe the whole thing was stupid."

"Maybe," Sally said, but she wasn't giving up.

While Louie sat thinking, she took a walk around the garage. She saw an old hockey stick and scrunched up her nose at it, then shook her head. She looked at the old bicycles . . . nothing there. She saw a beat-up croquet set. She shook her head at that, too. Then she saw something she'd never seen before. She lifted it out of the box and peered at it. It was a hard plastic small basket with a handle coming off the bottom, and an orange ball inside the basket.

"What's this?" she said.

Louie looked over. "Fling Ball," he said.

"What's Fling Ball?" She lifted out two large plastic baskets with handles. Louie picked up one of the baskets and showed her how it worked.

"You put a ball in here," said Louie, placing it in the basket. "Then you throw it." He flung the ball across the garage and it smacked the wall. They looked at each other and shrugged.

"Let's try it," she said. "Might work."

Finding a long strip of leather, Louie wrapped it around Marmalade's tail, then around the handle of the basket so that the basket became an extension of her tail. They stepped back and looked at Marmalade with her tail outstretched and the basket attached to it.

"It looks…ridiculous," said Louie.

"Here," said Sally, putting the ball into the basket. "Okay, girl, come on. Throw it, throw it."

Marmalade moved her tail a bit and the ball rolled out of the basket and went a few feet.

"Now, that's a ripper," said Louie.

"Let's go out onto the street."

So, with the basket dragging on the ground behind her, they took Marmalade out onto the street while Chester looked on from the sidewalk.

"How do we get her to throw it?" asked Louie.

"Easy," said Sally. "Food."

"Ah, food."

Louie ran inside and came back with some dog biscuits. He threw Sally a catcher's mitt. "You catch." Sally walked down about sixty feet—about the length from the pitcher's mound to home plate—and squatted down like a catcher.

"Okay, lay it in there, Marmy," she said, pounding her glove.

Marmalade stared at the dog biscuit Louie was holding over her head. Then Louie made a circle with it above her head and the dog started circling. And when the dog got going fast enough, Louie threw the biscuit. Marmalade's tail whipped around, and the ball came flying out of the basket and headed towards Sally—right at her. Sally's eyes got real big. It hit her catcher's glove so hard she fell backwards on the pavement. Louie raced over to her, just as she was sitting up.

"You okay?" he called.

"That was . . ." She sat up.

"What?"

"Not bad," she said.

"Not bad?" bellowed Louie. "It was a rocket!"

The next day, they went to the toy store and bought ten sets of Fling Ball, which they loaded into Al's pickup truck and took to the park, where each kid tied a basket to their dog's tail. It took a while, but when the dog biscuits came out, the kids got their dogs spinning and the balls came flying out of the Fling Ball baskets. At first, they flew all over the place, first way left, then way right, then behind them, then over the fence. It took them a while to get the right direction, but by lunchtime, the dogs could throw and catch using the baskets tied to their tails.

"But Louie . . . but Louie," all the kids yelled at once, gathering around. "They can't hit."

"And if they can't hit, they can't play," said Cara.

"I might have an idea for that," a voice said. They turned. It was Al, standing there with Mimi in her wheelchair, next to the truck.

"But first, who wants lunch?" Mimi said, holding up the picnic basket.

The kids all screamed and ran over, and Mimi wheeled her chair to the picnic table. Out of the picnic basket came tuna sandwiches, PB&J's, potatoes chips, pickles, peeled carrots, almonds, hard-boiled eggs, and juice boxes. The kids gobbled it all up like crazy. For dessert, Mimi handed out still-warm chocolate chip cookies. The kids wolfed them down too, wiping the chocolate off their hands onto their shirts.

"So, Dad," said Louie, "what's your idea?"

"I'll show you." Al went to his truck and brought back a bat and three pieces of insulation he got from the jobsite, the kind used for insulating pipes. Opening up the insulation hose, he slipped it over the end of the bat and wrapped the tape around it. Al then opened the insulation hose, wrapped it around Chester's tail, and put tape around it to hold it.

"Let's see if that works." The kids stepped back and watched. Chester just stood there, with a bat tied to his tail.

"How does he lift it?" said Donna.

"You make him spin," explained Al.

"Oh," said Louie. "I get it."

He patted Chester on the back and squatted down next to him. "Now, listen, boy. When you hear me whistle, you spin. Okay?" Louie didn't know if he understood, but he thought he'd try it.

Sally went to the mound. Louie put Chester in the batter's box and adjusted his feet. Chester looked up at him. Louie took a deep breath. Standing back, he nodded at Sally. She wound up and threw an easy pitch. Louie whistled. Nothing happened. Chester watched the ball go by.

"You gotta swing, boy," said Louie. "Just try it." He showed him how to do it and stepped back. Sally threw another one and Louie whistled. Chester didn't move, didn't swing, just looked over at Louie with a befuddled look on his face. "You gotta swing," repeated Louie. "Here, let me show you."

"Again," said Louie, after showing him, and Sally pitched and he let out a piercing whistle. This time Chester spun, and the bat came off the ground but missed the pitch by a mile.

"Okay, that's something," said Al.

"I don't know if this is going to work, Dad," said Louie

"Try again."

"Wait," said Levar, jumping in. "I got an idea." He took a dog biscuit and made a circle with it above Chester's head. Chester started to spin. "Now—throw it," yelled Levar. When Sally pitched, the ball came in and the bat came off the ground and crack, Chester hit a fly ball that landed in the soft grass in center field. Everyone watched it and then just stood there, frozen.

"Well, what do you know about that?" said Al.

"Again," yelled Sally.

It took a while, but Louie got the timing of the whistle down. Once Chester knew what was expected of him, he waited for the ball, heard the whistle, and spun around fast enough to get the bat off the ground.

He hit a fly ball, a few grounders, and after a while he was hitting line drives into the outfield.

"It works, Dad," Louie yelled in delight. "It works!"

It was time for the other dogs to take their turns. It took all day of spin and hit, spin and hit, spin and hit, before they could hit the ball most of the time. The kids had to work at teaching their dogs to spin using a dog biscuit, then time their whistle just right to get them to spin at the right time, then teach them to meet the ball with the bat. At first, they hit little grounders, then fly balls; then, when they got it down, line drives. Soon all the dogs were doing it.

"They can hit," said Cara, shaking her head. "Who knew?"

They practiced in the park every day for two whole weeks, the dogs getting better and better each day—hitting better, catching better, fielding better, throwing better. The kids worked out a series of whistle commands: one short whistle meant catch, two short whistles meant throw the ball to second, a long one meant touch the bag, and so on. Soon every kid learned all the commands, and each dog knew them, too.

"Okay, so the dogs can play baseball," said Sally, after practice one day. "So, what do we do now?"

Chapter Nine
THE DOGS WHO PLAY BASEBALL

They showed up the next day on the very same baseball field that Froggy had kicked them off of. With Sally in the lead, they marched right out onto the field in the middle of the game. Froggy was on the mound, about to pitch, when he saw them. He instantly pulled out his phone.

"I'm calling Animal Control," he said.

"Wait," said Louie.

"I told you—you can't play," said Froggy, dialing.

"*We're* not here to play, Dufus-face," said Sally.

"You're not?" He stopped dialing.

"We're not," said Louie. "But *they* are."

Scrunching up his face into wrinkles, Froggy looked around. "Who?" he asked.

"Them," said Louie.

"Them who?"

"The dogs."

"The dogs?"

"Yeah, the dogs," said Sally.

"The dogs? Those dogs?" asked Froggy, looking over at the Bulldog, German Shepherd, Scotty, Labrador and all the others sitting there looking on.

Louie stepped forward. "You said, when the dogs can play baseball, come on back and we'll play 'em. Isn't that what you said?"

"Uh, yeah, maybe, but . . ."

"So, we're back," said Sally. "And the dogs want to play you."

"Hey, guys, get a load of this," Froggy yelled to his players. "They want us to play the dogs."

Everybody broke up. "They want us to play a bunch of dogs."

"Yep, one game," said Louie. "Winner gets the field."

"We already got the field," said Froggy.

"Right, we thought of that," said Sally. "So we'll bet . . . these." She held up her cell phone. The rest of the kids held up their cell phones, too.

"You're betting your phones?" asked Froggy. "On a bunch of dogs?"

"Yep."

"On dogs?" he repeated.

"How many times do we have to say it, Froggy? I know you're dense and all, so take it or leave it," said Sally.

Froggy looked back at his teammates. They all nodded, like *yeah, we'll take their phones.*

"Okay," said Froggy. "We'll play your stupid dogs."

"All right!" yelled Louie. "Game on."

The kids ran to the dugout to get their dogs ready, and the dogs lined up, tossed some balls back and forth and took some practice swings. Froggy and his team just stared in astonishment.

"What's the matter?" yelled Sally. "Never seen dogs play baseball before?"

Froggy and his teammates just stood there, blinking hard. "What's your name?" he called.

"What?" said Louie.

"Your team name," said Froggy. "What's your team name?"

"Oh." Louie looked at Sally and shrugged. Louie thought for a moment and yelled back, "The Bronx Barkers."

"Oh, man, nobody's gonna believe this," wailed Froggy, shaking his head.

"And you're the Bronx Bullies," yelled back Sally.

Froggy took the mound. "Let's get this over with."

Chester was the lead-off hitter, so Louie taped the bat to his tail, and Chester walked slowly up to the plate, dragging the bat behind him. Froggy couldn't believe his eyes. Chester stepped into the batter's box, set his feet, picked up one foot, shook it, picked up the other, shook it, and got set—with the bat behind him. Froggy just stood there.

"You gonna pitch?" yelled Sally.

Froggy shook himself, shrugged, wound up, and threw a fastball down and away. Louie whistled. Chester spun. The bat came up and connected perfectly with the pitch, sending a line drive into right field. The pudgy round-faced right fielder was so amazed he let it go right by him without even trying to catch it. Chester raced for first, heard the whistle, rounded the bag, and headed for second. By this time, the right fielder had chased down the ball. He threw it into second. Sally whistled from third base. Chester heard the whistle, slid in, and beat the throw.

"What the—?" stammered Froggy, raising his upper lip.

"You ain't seen nothin' yet," Sally yelled.

"Time," yelled Veronica, and she ran out and took the bat off Chester's tail.

Gabby the Bassett Hound was up next. She wouldn't go up to the plate unless she got a treat, so Louie said, "Give her a treat," and Veronica did. Then Gabby went up to the plate. Froggy looked in, lowering his head lower, lower, and lower still, because the dog was so short, then shook it off, straightened up and pitched. Veronica whistled. Gabby spun and hit a ground ball down the third base line. The third baseman lunged for it, but it got under his mitt. Louie whistled, and Chester bolted from second. Louie waved him in, and he scored.

"Give that dog a treat," said Louie.

"There's more where that came from," yelled Sally, from across the infield.

Bernie the Bernese Mountain Dog came up next. He hit a towering fly ball to center, and the whole team rose to their feet, hoping for a home run. But it fell short, and the center fielder caught it on the warning track.

"Ohhhhhhhhhhh," they all groaned, sitting back down.

"Oh, well," said Sally. "Next time."

Champ the Collie struck out. Donut hit a grounder to second for an easy out, and the inning was over. Score: Barkers 1-Bullies 0. As they came off the field, Louie looked over at the fence and saw a few spectators crowding in. "Looks like we got some fans," he said.

"Really?" asked Sally, looking over.

"Okay, let's get out there," said Louie.

The dogs ran out onto the field… Pal the Great Dane in center, Oscar the German Shepherd in right, Champ the Collie in left field, Donut the Mutt at short, Bull the Bulldog at third, Pearl the Scotty at second, and Chester at first. Bernie the Bernese Mountain Dog played catcher and got down behind home plate. Marmalade walked slowly to the mound, dragging the Fling

Ball basket tied to her tail. When she got there, she turned around and looked at Sally.

"You got this, girl," Sally said softly.

Marmalade set herself. Sally whistled. Marmalade whipped around, and the ball came tearing out of the basket towards home plate. It flew right by the batter and Bernie caught it in his basket. He whipped it back to Marmalade. The batter, a tall kid with bad teeth and black hair covering his ears, backed away from home plate, looked over at Froggy, and pushed up his shoulders.

"What's the matter?" yelled Froggy back. "Never seen a dog throw a fastball before?"

"No!" wailed the kid.

"Well, just get back in there."

Marmalade wound up and threw another pitch. The batter watched it go by for a strike. He turned again to Froggy, who yelled for him to get back in there. This time the batter swung at the pitch, hitting a line drive into center field for a single. From the dugout, Froggy let out a sigh of relief. "Okay, that's more like it."

But the next boy hit a ground ball to Pearl at second. She came up with it, flipped it with her mouth over to Donut covering second, who caught it in her basket and whipped it to Chester at first for the double play.

"What the—?" yelled Froggy.

"This ain't gonna be as easy as we thought," said one of his teammates.

"We can't lose to a bunch of dogs," Froggy moaned.

Several more spectators lined the fence line to watch, and some took out their phones and snapped some photos of the game.

In the next inning, Bull the Bulldog hit a double to left field, and Bernie bunted him to third. Marmalade hit a sacrifice fly to right field, scoring Bull from third.

"What the—?" yelled Froggy. Juan climbed up and changed the scoreboard: Barkers 2 Bullies 0.

Froggy and the Bullies came up next inning and got a rally going. They hit a double to left, a single to center, an infield single, and scored a run. Barkers 2-Bullies 1.

But the Bronx Barkers—the dogs—broke it open in the fifth inning with four runs, with hits from Oscar the German Shepherd, Donut the Mutt, Pearl the Scotty, and a triple from Chester, making it Barkers 6-Bullies 1. The score stayed that way until Froggy's team, the Bullies, came up in the bottom of the ninth.

"Three more outs," said Sally, unable to contain herself. Marmalade struck out the first batter. "Two more outs," said Sally excitedly.

The next Bullies hitter smashed a line drive down the first base line, and Chester leaped high in the air and snagged it on the fly. The dugout erupted in cheers.

"Way to go, Chester," called Louie.

"One more out," said Sally. And she crossed her fingers behind her back.

As the next Bullies hitter walked up to the plate, Louie yelled, "Time," and he and Sally went out to the mound to talk to Marmalade.

"One more out, and we've won the game," said Sally.

"Right," said Louie.

"So why are we out here?" she said.

"Because that's what managers do. They go to the mound."

"Oh, brother," she said.

"Give her a treat, and let's win this." Sally gave Marmy a treat and they went back to the dugout.

Froggy was up. He walked to the plate, his eyes flaring. He tapped the plate with his bat. Marmalade wound up and threw a fastball. Froggy swung and hit a fly ball to center field. Froggy's dugout erupted in cheers when the ball left the bat, like it was the greatest hit ever.

"That's it," said Sally, watching the ball come down. "Easy out." Pal the Great Dane moved in to make the catch, then stopped and looked around in confusion.

"What's going on?" yelled Sally. "Catch it. Catch it."

But Froggy's teammates were yelling so loud, Pal couldn't hear.

"She can't hear the whistle," said Louie. "They're too loud."

Chip whistled louder and louder, but Pal couldn't hear it, no matter what. The ball dropped in front of the Great Dane, who then wandered up to it and sniffed it calmly, while everyone in the dugout yelled to him.

Froggy rounded first and headed to second, picking up speed. On his way to second, he saw Pal the Great Dane pick up the ball and trot the wrong way into the outfield. So, he kept going, rounding second and heading for third base. Pal, unaware of the commotion, just curled up with the ball and went to sleep. Froggy rounded third and ran for home.

"Uh-oh," said Louie.

"You can say that again," said Sally.

His teammates ran to the plate and hugged Froggy as he got home. "We got 'em now," yelled Froggy. "We got 'em now."

The next batter hit a lame bunt, but Froggy and his team yelled and screamed, making such a racket the dogs couldn't hear the commands. The next batter hit a ground ball to Pearl the Scotty at second, but since she couldn't hear the whistle, she let the ball go by and then ran in for a treat.

"Uh-oh," said Sally.

"You can say that again," said Louie.

Froggy's team scored one run, then another; then they pulled ahead and beat the dogs 7-6. Sally and her whole team lined up, heads down, and dropped their cell phones into Froggy's hat.

"My dad's gonna kill me," said Chuck.

"Mine, too," said Donna.

"This is all my fault," said Louie, watching the kids drop their phones into the hat.

"Not all, just most," Sally replied, with a slight smile.

"Thanks," he said.

"How about a rematch?" yelled Sally to Froggy.

"No way," said Froggy. "We ain't playing *them* again."

Louie and the kids slowly made their way off the field. Mr. Park stood at the fence line with a bag of oranges, giving one out to each kid and dog biscuits to the dogs.

"It's okay, dogs win next time," he said.

"There isn't going to be a next time, Mr. Park," said Sally, sadly.

"Dogs play baseball," said Mr. Park. "I saw them. Dogs play."

Louie and Chester, Sally and Marmalade all walked out of Van Cortland Park and onto Bayside Avenue. They walked slowly, heads down, saying nothing. It was shaping up to be a long walk home, with lots of explaining to do about how they lost their cell phones, and calls to parents and, well, a lot of bad stuff. Louie didn't speak. Sally, who really didn't care that she lost her phone, just walked along checking out the bagel shops. Just then, a neighborhood kid, a girl about ten, came walking towards them. When she saw them, she stopped and her eyes grew wide. "Is that Chester?" she blurted out. "Is that really him?"

"Uh, yeah, that's Chester," said Louie. "Why?"

"Can I get a selfie?" the girl asked.

"Sure. If you want."

The girl got down next to Chester and took a selfie. "Good game," she said. "You almost won." And she ran off.

"How do you…?" Louie called after her, but she was off.

"What was that?" asked Sally.

"Not sure," said Louie, shrugging. They kept walking down Bayside Avenue. Another neighborhood boy ran by and yelled back at them, "Good pitching, Marmalade."

"What's going on?" Louie took off his baseball hat and rubbed his head.

They kept walking. A bunch of neighborhood kids from the playground looked up and saw the dogs and came running over. "Chester!" they yelled. "Marmalade!" They surrounded the dogs, took pictures and took selfies.

"What's going on?" wondered Sally.

"I don't know," he said.

And just then Cara came running down the street after them, with Donut loping by her side.

"We're trending," she screamed. "I just saw it. Those people watching the game posted pictures."

"We're trending???" said Sally.

"Hashtag the dogs who play baseball. We're famous," said Cara.

"Huh," said Sally.

When they turned the corner to Louie's street, there was a crowd milling in front of his house.

"Holy Moly," said Louie. "Look!"

"There they are," someone from the crowd yelled. And the crowd came running down the street towards them.

"What do we do?" asked Louie.

Sally put her arm around Marmalade and kneeled down. "Photo op," she yelled. "Photo op."

The crowd surged in, petting Chester and Marmalade, and taking selfies and photos with Chester and Louie, then Sally and Marmalade, then with all four of them, then a closeup of Chester's paw. Finally, Louie had to put his arm around Chester's neck and make a path through the crowd to his front door. The crowd chanted, "CHEST-ER, CHEST-ER," and then, "MAR-MA-LADE. MAR-MA-LADE."

Al came out onto the porch, pushing Mimi in her wheelchair, and she looked down at Louie in the crowd and mouthed, "What's this?" Louie just raised his shoulders, put his arms out and mouthed back, "I don't know."

"Oh, my," said his mother, watching the crowd take photos of the dogs. "Oh, my."

"CHEST-ER, CHEST-ER," chanted the crowd.

Chapter Ten
THE RENT

In a skyscraper on Eighth Avenue in Manhattan, on the eighteenth story, in a shabby office, at a beat-up desk, sitting in a worn-out swivel chair, was a young woman with a giant head of black hair, shiny red lipstick, a Tiffany gold necklace, a Versace silk blouse, a Prada skirt, Jimmy Choo high heels, and a new ring on her wedding finger. She sat at her desk painting her nails (red, of course) while playing solitaire on the computer with the one finger that wasn't painted yet. The plaque on her desk said ACCOUNT EXECUTIVE, and the name on the frosted glass door, backwards, read EDWARD ANTONETTI, PUBLIC RELATIONS. Eddie was, technically at least, her boss, and also the man she planned on marrying. Which is why she wore the ring, although Eddie didn't have the money for the ring she wanted, so she wore "this curtain ring," as she called it, until he could afford the one she really wanted. Her job at the company was to handle the media, send out press releases, contact clients, arrange press conferences, set up events, pitch reporters, basically to do everything needed at a PR company. But now she spent her time doing her nails and planning a wedding she wasn't even sure they could have because they had no clients, no money, and Eddie didn't want to take money from her parents, who were loaded. So she basically did—zip, because there was nothing to do. She played solitaire. And painted her nails.

It was a two-room office, with her up front at her desk, and a waiting area next to her desk that no one ever sat in, and an office in the back where Edward (who everyone called Eddie) worked. He was in the back office now, probably looking out the window. Her office was nothing to shout about. It had paint peeling off the wall here and there. Her furniture consisted of a metal desk with a Formica top, three folding chairs, one very old filing cabinet with a broken lock, a computer from the Stone Age, and a carpet that caught her Jimmy Choo heels just about every time she walked around. She swore when she caught a heel, but she was a good Catholic girl, so she always swore quietly so no one would hear.

Suddenly, there was a knock at the door. She looked up. No one ever came by. They had no clients, so it couldn't be that. She eyed the door warily. Through the frosted glass she could see a figure, and it looked like a man in a dark suit, but she couldn't tell for sure. She kind of hoped he'd go away so she just sat there watching. He knocked again.

She blew on her freshly painted nails, got up, and walked across the carpeted floor, caught her heel, almost fell, swore—softly—and stopped next to the door. The figure was gone now, and she could see nothing through the frosted glass. Then she heard the mail flap go up and looked down. Someone was looking in. She flung open the door and looked down and there was a man on his knees on the floor outside the door.

"Can I help you?" she said, in a frosty tone.

The man got up off his knees. He was middle aged, balding, a bit paunchy, in a black suit and white shirt with no tie. "I'm looking for Edward Antonetti," he said.

"He's not available. Can I help you?"

"You might want to give him this." He held out a plain white envelope for her to take. She backed away from it. "I'm from the building," he explained.

"That's nice. I'm from Queens."

He gave her an annoyed look. "I mean, I'm the building agent, and it's my job to collect the rents, and this is for Eddie." He held out the envelope again, but she crossed her arms and did not touch it. He said, "Look, you gotta pay your rent or we're going to have to kick you out."

"You'll have to take that up with Eddie," she said, pushing the door closed. The building agent stuck his foot in the door and smiled tightly, not a real smile but a tough guy smile.

"You work with him, huh? With Eddie, I mean."

"I do. We're also engaged to be married if you must know, but yeah, he's my boss."

"Is he here?"

"No, he's out."

"Where?"

"Out."

"Out, like in his office?" He tried to push past her, but she blocked him. "Okay, look," he said, "you haven't paid your rent in five months."

"That's news to me," she replied. She stood there with a fixed smile that said, *is there anything else I can help you with?*

"Look, here's how it works. People take offices here, it's an office building. They pay rent. Then they get to stay. Got it? You are staying but not paying. Got that? So you got to pay or you can't stay."

"Eddie," she said. "Take it up with him."

"We won't wait forever," he warned. "He has to pay the rent."

"I'm sure it's just an oversight. I'll bring it up with him as soon as he gets back," she said.

The building agent gave her a serious look. "You got ten days, or you're out," he said.

"And by that, you mean . . .what?"

"Out! Like on the street. I don't care where you go, but you're out."

"Mr. Antonetti is out on a very important assignment, but I'll tell him when he comes back," she said, shutting the door on him.

"Ten days," he yelled through the door. "If you don't come up with the money, you're out."

She listened as he walked away. When he was gone, she turned and put her back to the door and took a deep breath. She walked back to her desk and opened the calendar. It was empty—no appointments booked at all. She pulled up the call log. No phone messages—none. Heaving a sigh, she got up and walked into Eddie's office.

"Eddie?" she said, entering the office. She looked around. It was empty. "Eddie, where are you? Eddie?"

"Is he gone?" said a voice from under the desk.

"Eddie!" she sighed, exasperated.

"Is he gone?"

"Yes, he's gone."

Eddie Antonetti came out from under the desk, stood up, and dusted himself off. Eddie was a handsome man—tall, dark-haired, olive-skinned, thirty-two years old, in a well-tailored light grey suit with a striped shirt and red tie, black wingtip shoes, maroon socks, and a purple and black silk square flaring out of his breast pocket. Being under the desk had rumpled his suit, so he smoothed it, along with his beautiful head of black hair, which he re-shaped in the mirror.

"Eddie, they're gonna throw us out," she exclaimed, in her very very New York accent. "You gotta pay the rent. If you don't pay, we're out."

"Don't worry about it," he said.

"That's what you always say—*don't worry about it*. But *I am* worried about it."

"I'll take care of it."

"That's what you always say, *I'll take care of it*. But you don't."

"I will. I said I will, and I will."

"But how, Eddie? We have no business. Nobody's calling. We have no clients, not even any maybe clients. No one knows we exist, and no one's going to hire us. We're just slowly sinking. Sinking, Eddie, sinking. Did you hear me, *we're sinking*."

"Yeah, you said we're sinking."

"Right, 'cause we are."

"We're not sinking," said Eddie.

"We're *sinking*," she repeated.

"I'll take care of it."

"I'm calling my parents," she said, heading back to her office.

"No!" he said.

"Why not?" She stopped.

"I'm not getting married owing your parents money, that's why."

She put her hands on her hips, eyed him sideways, gave him a cold stare and said, "You may not be getting married at all, at this rate, if you know what I mean." She turned her back on him and walked out of the room.

"I have to get back to work," he called after her.

"What work?" she called back. "We don't have any work."

She sat back down at her desk. "I'm calling my parents," she yelled.

"No, you're not," yelled back Eddie.

"We're broke, Eddie, broke."

"I'll take care of it," Eddie shot back.

"Ah!" she exclaimed. *"Eddie!!!"*

He didn't respond, so she plopped down at her desk. Sick of playing solitaire, she picked up her cell phone and started scrolling through her feed. A cat video caught her eye, and she watched it. She picked up her nail polish brush, about to paint her last nail when she scrolled by a photo of a Bulldog and a smile broke out that lit up her face.

"Hey, get a load of this," she said, walking back into Eddie's office.

"What?" he said sourly.

"On my feed—look. Some kids in the Bronx taught their dogs how to play baseball."

She showed Eddie the phone, and Eddie took a quick look and turned away. "Stupid," he said. "All that stuff on the Internet, it's stupid."

"Yeah, but it's kinda cute," she said, smiling while scrolling through the photos. "Look, they actually played a game. And oh, my God, they almost won." Another photo of Pearl the Scottish Terrier popped up on her screen. "Sooooo cute."

"Stop looking at all that stuff," complained Eddie. "We got work to do."

"Okay," she said, still smiling, as she walked back to her office. "But it's awfully sweet. You'd see that, if you weren't such a grump."

Eddie threw open his laptop, determined to find something to do. He checked his To Do list, but there was nothing on it. He checked his day planner with the heading, HABITS FOR HIGHLY SUCCESSFUL PEOPLE. He had nothing on it. He made a face and moved on. Eventually, he found his way to his feed and checked his page. He scrolled down. And then, there it was, THE DOGS WHO PLAY BASEBALL, right there on his feed. "Stupid," he muttered aloud. "Dogs playing baseball—so dumb." He scrolled down, then stopped, there was something about it… then he scrolled back up to the dogs. He played the video of Chester hitting a single, rounding first.

"What the—?" He watched another clip. This one had a ground ball hit to Pearl the Scotty, who caught it, tagged second for the force out and whipped the ball to first for the out.

"A double play—?" he mused.

The next clip showed Pal the Great Dane making a spectacular catch in center field and throwing out the runner trying to tag up.

"You gotta be kidding me," he said. "Dogs playing baseball?"

"What did you say?" said Andrea, coming back through the door.

"Nothing," he said.

"What are you looking at?"

"Nothing." He turned his laptop away.

"You're watching the dogs, aren't you? I told you they were cute."

"No, it's stupid." He slammed the laptop shut.

"Okay, but people like that stuff. It makes them feel good."

"I gotta get back to work."

"Okay," she said and went back to her office, still scrolling through the videos.

Eddie picked up his yellow pad. And pen. Then without thinking, he wrote, "DOGS WHO PLAY BASEBALL."

He looked at it. Something went off in his brain. He stared at the photos of the game. He looked at his yellow pad and the words, DOGS WHO PLAY BASE-

BALL. In a violent heave, he pushed back his chair and rose.

"Andrea!" he yelled. "Andrea!"

"What?" she said, calmly, appearing in the doorway a moment later.

"Dogs!" he yelled.

"Yeah, what about them?"

"Don't you see, dogs!!!"

"See what?" she said.

"The dogs—play baseball," he shouted.

"Yeah, I told you they did," she said. "So what?"

"Don't you see?"

"See what? I see a bunch of dogs playing baseball. What's to see?"

"Let's go," he said, grabbing his briefcase and running for the door.

"Where are we going?"

"Come on." He raced out. "COME ON!"

"Eddie," she sighed, grabbing her Dolce & Gabbana purse, her car keys, and her phone off her desk.

"Hurry!"

"Okay, I'm coming, all right?" she yelled back. "Just hold your horses, would ya!!!"

Chapter Eleven
HEY KID, GOT AN AGENT?

An hour later, Andrea eased her Mercedes Benz into the parking lot at Van Cortland Park and brought it to a stop, looking out onto the baseball field.

"So, this is nature," she said, her gaze sweeping the park. "Who knew?"

"It's not nature," said Eddie. "It's the Bronx."

"Oh."

Eddie looked out on the field. It took him a minute to focus, but soon he could see the dogs at their positions, three outfielders, a dog playing first, a dog at second, another at short, another at third. Crack! Bull the Bulldog hit a sharp line drive into the gap in left center and rounded first, dug for second, and slid in for a double.

"Holy Moly," shouted Eddie. "Did you see that?"

Andrea rolled her eyes. "Yeah, I saw it. Can we go now?"

Eddie got out of the car and walked to the fence.

"I'm hungry," she yelled. He didn't even turn around. "You know how I get when I get hungry." He didn't turn around. She sighed.

She got out of the car and followed him to the fence in her four-inch stiletto Jimmy Choo shoes, and all the while her heels cut into the grass and dug down deep into the dirt. "Ow, ow, ow, ow," she moaned. "Eddie!" He didn't answer. He stood at the fence and watched the game. Looking to his right, he saw Froggy and his whole team sitting in the bleachers, mesmerized, watching the dogs play. Looking to his left, he saw Mr. Park in his apron watching the game, holding a bag. He looked back at the game. Marmalade wound up and threw, and Donut whiffed.

"You see that?" said Eddie. "A strikeout."

"Yeah, I saw it," said Andrea, with a smirk. "It made my day."

Oscar the German Shepherd bunted down the third-base line. Bull fielded it and threw to first to get the out by a step.

"Holy Moly," said Eddie. "It's real baseball."

"You've said that, yeah."

"Don't you get it?" Eddie asked, turning to her.

"They're cute—but who cares? We got a business to run...or try to run anyway."

Champ the Collie hit a grounder through the hole into right field and took first. And Chester came around to score.

"Look, they're *actually* playing baseball!" Eddie exclaimed.

"Right, can we go now?"

Ignoring her, he said, "come on" and took a seat in the bleachers. Andrea hobbled over in her high heels, almost falling, and sat down next to him. Eddie kept his eyes glued to the game.

"Don't we have better things to do than hang around with a bunch of dogs?" she said.

The dogs got the last out, and the game was over. The kids and dogs rounded up their gear and wandered off. Louie and Sally grabbed their bags, put leashes on Chester and Marmalade, and came out of the dugout, heading off.

"Hey, kid," said Eddie.

Louie looked over. "Yeah?"

"Got an agent?"

Louie looked over at Sally, like, *what did he just say?*

They met that evening in Louie's house, all of them— kids and dogs and parents—crammed into the tiny living room. Al and Mimi set out platters of cheese and crackers. Louie and Sally brought chairs from all over the house, including the folding chairs from the garage. Eddie and Andrea sat on the couch, and everyone faced them. Even the dogs sat quietly at attention. All eyes were on Eddie.

"This could be the biggest thing this city has ever seen," exclaimed Eddie.

"Do you really think so?" asked Mimi, skeptically.

"It will be huge. HUGE!"

"Huge?" said Mimi. "Really?"

"I mean, they're just dogs," said Al.

"Not just dogs," replied Eddie, gesturing. "Dogs *who play baseball.*"

"Yeah—but will anyone really care?" asked Sally.

Eddie stood up. "Look, you got something that no one's ever seen before. Never. Ever. No one's ever seen dogs play baseball, and they're gonna go crazy."

"My," said Mimi.

"I don't know," said Al. "They're just dogs."

"And kids," added Mimi, with a note of caution.

"Mr. Cohen, Mrs. Cohen, and all of you," said Eddie. "Listen . . . This is a once in a lifetime opportunity. It may never come along again."

"What *exactly* do you want to do?" said Mimi, shooting a nervous look at Al.

"Make them famous. Really famous. The Dogs Who Play Baseball. Let the whole world know."

"How?"

"The media!" he said. "TV, radio, cable, newspapers, social media—they'll be everywhere."

"You want the dogs to go on TV?" asked Mimi.

Al thought for a moment, then shook his head, "I don't think so, Mr. Antonetti."

"Sorry, Mr. Antonetti, but thanks for coming," said Mimi.

"All right," said Eddie, flopping back on the sofa. "I understand. Really, I do. It's just that we could have made a fortune on this."

"Money?" said Louie, perking up. "We can make money?"

"Oh, sure," said Eddie, rising again. "Kid, we can make more money than you've ever dreamed of."

"How much?" asked Louie.

"How much?"

"Yeah, how much can we make?" said Louie.

"Well, it's hard to say . . ."

"Five hundred and twenty-nine thousand dollars?" asked Louie.

"Well, sure, yeah, that and a lot more," said Eddie.

"Louie, let's not—" said Mimi.

"Then, we're in," Louie said. He looked over at his team. They nodded. "Okay," said he, "we're in."

"So, Eddie, you're the genius, what do we do now?" asked Sally.

"Well," said Eddie, "I'm glad you asked."

Chapter Twelve
MAGGIE HART

This was, after all, Manhattan—land of sky-scrapers, land of office buildings and restaurants and Broadway and Wall Street and Times Square, and billboards and yellow cabs and horns blaring and lots and lots of traffic. Land of nightclubs and Radio City Music Hall and the Empire State Building. Land of promises and golden dreams. Oh, and land of newspapers.

And that's where they were right now, Louie, Sally, and Eddie, standing outside the fifty-story office building for the NEW YORK POST. They were across the street, looking up, and up, and up, and up at the building, till the skyscraper kissed the sky. *The Post*. This was where it got made. The whole building, all fifty stories, was the newspaper, with floor after floor of printing presses, stacking machines, rolls of newsprint, copywriters, editors, reporters—everything and *everyone* needed to put out the paper. Over in the alley they could see the delivery trucks parked on the curb, waiting for the next day's paper to be loaded before delivering it all over the city. The building took up one whole block, with traffic noisily whizzing by. And the people—there was an endless stream of people coming and going through the revolving doors in and out of the building.

Louie gulped aloud. "We're going in there?" said he.

"Yep," said Eddie, his voice shaking a tiny bit.

Sally turned to him. "You've been in there before, right? I mean, this is not your first time?"

"Sure," he said, "I been there, sure." He paused and then said, "when I was on a field trip in fifth grade."

"That's reassuring," said Sally.

"Come on," he said.

They crossed Eighth Avenue and went through the revolving door into the lobby. A security guard stood at the desk next to a turnstile they had to go through. "I'll do the talking," said Eddie. "You gotta be tough to get in." He stepped up to the guard. "Maggie Hart," he said gruffly.

"You're here to see Maggie Hart?" the guard said.

"That's what I said, Maggie Hart."

The guard checked the sheet. "Got an appointment?"

"We got a story for her," said Eddie.

"Ninth floor," said the guard, opening the gate.

They were in. They took the elevator up, and when it opened onto the ninth floor, they stepped out into a filthy corridor with broken lights with shards of glass hanging overhead, old boxes stacked in the hallway brimming with old phones, a broken water fountain wrapped in plastic, a scuffed floor, and an old bulletin board. They stepped up to the directory. Most of the letters had fallen out. "Look," said Sally. Some new letters spelled out "M. Hart 427." Eddie checked the numbers on the wall with arrows. "Come on," he said, "this way." They made their way down the hall, dodging old computers stacked up, garbage overflowing from the cans, and stacks of old newspapers. Eddie stopped in front of Room 427.

"Nice place you brought us to," said Sally.

"This must be it," he said, looking around. But his voice wasn't so sure.

"Who we going to see, Pig Pen?"

He knocked.

"Yeah"—a female voice answered from inside—"come in."

The door made a scraping sound as it opened. They went in. The office was not much better than the hallway, with boxes stacked in the corner, Styrofoam cups turned on their sides on the desk, old coffee stains on the chair, a pile of old computer equipment, cables coiled everywhere, chipped paint on the walls, and a ripped carpet. A woman sitting at a metal desk looked up. She was blonde and pretty, in a rough kind of way, with an expression that said, *What the heck do you want?* She had her hair pulled back and a pen stuck behind her ear. She had on jeans, a New York Yankees shirt and old running shoes. The room had an odor of old shoes—or old newspapers—Louie couldn't tell which.

"Are you Maggie Hart?" asked Eddie.

"Used to be," she replied gruffly.

"You cover the Yankees?"

"Not anymore," she said. "What can I do for you?"

"I'm Eddie Antonetti, I'm a PR guy, and this is Louie Cohen and Sally Cartwright, from the Bronx."

"The Bronx, huh?"

"We have a story for you."

"A story, huh? You and everybody else in the city, and most of them aren't worth it."

"It may be the biggest story of your career," said Eddie.

She shook her head. "Okay, look—want to know why I'm in this lovely office? Nice, huh? Well, I'll tell ya. I wrote a story that said the Yankees were moving to New Jersey. Yeah, Jersey. As in *New Jersey*."

"The Yankees are moving to New Jersey?" blurted out Louie.

"That's the problem—they aren't. But I wrote a story that said they were. I had a source, a good source, but it turned out I had it wrong. Dead wrong. I got nailed to the cross. They almost fired me. I kinda wish they had. Instead, I got moved to this beautiful office, with no stories to write—no work—and everyone in the building thinks I'm a loser. So, here's a tip for you.

If you have a good story, you might want to give it to somebody else."

"But you're Maggie Hart," said Eddie.

"Yeah, not anymore."

"You want it or not?"

"All right, you've been warned," said Maggie, shrugging. "So, what is it?"

"We can tell you," said Sally. "But . . ."

"We have to show you," said Louie.

She looked at Louie, then at Sally, then at Eddie, with an expression that said, *what are you getting me into here?*

"Not much keeping you here," said Eddie, motioning to the door.

An hour later, they stood along the fence line at Van Cortland Park, where the dogs were playing a game. *Crack!* Donut hit a line drive to center. *Crack!* Chester hit a fly ball to right. *Crack!* Pearl hit a grounder down the left field line.

"You gotta be kidding me, right?" said Maggie, turning back to them. "You want me to do a story about a bunch of dogs?"

"Yep," said Eddie.

"Dogs playing baseball?"

"That's right," said Louie.

"Listen, you seem like okay guys, so here's the deal. I'm already a laughingstock," she said. "And if I write a story about a bunch of dogs playing baseball, that'll cinch it."

"It's not just a bunch of dogs," corrected Sally.

"It's a bunch of dogs who really *play baseball*," said Louie.

"I'll be laughed out of the newsroom," said Maggie.

"At least consider it," said Eddie.

"Okay." She paused. "Okay, I considered it and the answer is no."

"We're playing a game on Saturday," said Eddie.

"Against who, a bunch of cats?" said Maggie. Louie and Sally burst out laughing, and Maggie, smiling, turned to Eddie and said, "Hey, they're my best audience."

"Ms. Hart," said Louie.

"Yes?"

"There are two things people like, baseball and—"

"Dogs," said Maggie.

"And we have both," he said.

"It could turn your career around," said Eddie. "You could get the Yankees back."

"With this? Fat chance."

Maggie looked out at the field and saw the dogs playing, and they weren't bad, she thought to herself. She knew it could mean the end of her career, the dumb sports reporter who wrote about dogs playing baseball. But if these dogs could actually play, it might just work.

She turned to them. "You got a manager for these mutts?" she said.

Louie turned to Sally, with a look that said, *we haven't thought about that.*

"Well, we're gonna need one," said Maggie. "You don't got a team without a manager."

Chapter Thirteen
GREATEST PLACE ON EARTH

The greatest of all ballparks, the greatest of all stadiums, the greatest of all sporting venues, the greatest of all places on Planet Earth, as everyone knows, is Yankee Stadium—in the Bronx, New York, a stone's throw from the Major Deegan Expressway, along the banks of the Harlem River and on the other side of the river from the upper tip of the great borough of Manhattan at One Hundred Fifty-ninth Street. Yankee Stadium was built in 1923, and what all Yankee fans know, the Yankee Stadium of today is not the original, but a new stadium opened in 2009, built to look as much as possible like the old stadium. Everything—the seats, the field, and the bleachers—was built to resemble the old stadium, and it was built only a block away. After they finished building the new stadium, they tore down the old one and made it into a park. So, when a red Ferrari drove into the stadium parking lot, it parked next to the new stadium that looked like the old stadium and that still ranked as one of the greatest places on Earth.

The license plate of the Ferrari read ARCH. Out of the car popped the soon-to-be Hall of Famer, but now retired, Yankee great, shortstop Dexter Archer, dressed in a flashy blue suit, with a red-and-black tie, and wearing a New York Yankees baseball cap. Archer played twenty Major League Baseball seasons for the Yankees. And as they say, once a Yankee, always a Yankee.

The Yankees were on the road today, playing a three-game series against Cleveland, so the place was pretty much deserted except for some workmen repainting the lines in the parking lot. The workmen saw Archer and yelled, "Hey, Arch," and he waved back and flashed that million-dollar smile. The workers chanted: "HALL OF FAME, HALL OF FAME." Archer's smile grew even bigger, and he gave them a backwards wave as he went through the gate into the stadium. Archer played for the Yankees till he was forty years old, and since then he wanted to do one thing and one thing only, which is why he was at Yankee Stadium on this beautiful summer's day in a business suit, wearing his Yankees cap.

He walked past the concessions and up the ramp to the field level. Archer stopped and took it all in. He saw the outfield and the perfectly manicured grass, cut crosswise in alternating strips; he saw the infield dirt, smooth and brushed; and he saw his spot at shortstop where he fielded thousands of ground balls and caught countless line drives. He saw home plate, where he got many of his 2,459 hits over his career for a lifetime .331 batting average, and his 410 home runs. He had 9,150 at-bats over his career, played in 10 All Star games, won three World Series, and was American League Rookie of the Year. He looked up into the rafters and saw his number, 27, hanging there, retired forever, which meant no one else was ever going to wear that number again, and he had a plaque there at the stadium.

"Heya, Dex!" said a voice behind him, and he turned to see General Manager Fritz McComber stretching out his hand.

"Hi, Fritz," he said. They shook hands and then both looked out over the field.

"Like you remember it?"

"Yeah, pretty much."

"You miss it?" asked Fritz, then waved him off. "Of course, you do. Everybody does when it's over. Come on, the guys all want to say hi."

Fritz had a round face and a bald head and wore a simple blue polo shirt with a small Yankees logo over the breast pocket. Leading Archer along the concourse, they went up the elevator and down a long hallway to the management offices. When he walked in, everyone in the office rose, especially the young guys and gals who worked in the "bullpen," the big open office space on the floor. They mobbed him till Fritz stepped in. "Okay, break it up. We got a meeting." He led Archer into the conference room, where two other guys, Head Scout Andy Toledo and Assistant GM Paul Atkins were waiting.

"Dexter, you know Andy?"

"Sure," said Archer, shaking hands.

"And Paul," said Fritz.

"Hi, Paul," said Archer. "Good to see you."

"Have a seat, Dexter, have a seat." They sat around the large oval conference table—Archer on one side and Fritz, Andy, and Paul on the other, looking across the table at him.

"I'm glad you called," said Fritz. Archer nodded. "It's always good to bring the guys back, isn't it?" Andy and Paul nodded. "So, tell us, what can we do for you, Dexter?" said Fritz.

"Well . . ." Archer leaned forward, nervously knitting his fingers together. "As you know, I've been out of baseball for two years now—"

"Yeah, but the fans still love you, Dexter," said Fritz, pointing at him. "They're crazy about you, aren't they, guys?" The guys nodded.

"And I've been doing a lot of thinking—" continued Archer.

"Always dangerous for a retired guy," said Andy, chuckling. The guys laughed along with him. Archer didn't laugh.

"And I know now what I want to do," he said.

"And what's that?" Paul asked.

"I want to manage."

Fritz, Andy, and Paul just stared back at him. So, Archer went on. "I think, that if given the chance, I could make a good manager—"

Fritz cut him off. "Dexter, have you thought about this?" he said roughly.

Archer took a deep breath and went on. "I have. I've thought about it a lot and—"

Andy interrupted. "Dexter, just because you played for eighteen years—"

"Twenty."

"Right, twenty. That doesn't mean you can manage."

"Dexter, it's like this," Fritz said very slowly, carefully, as if he were talking to a child. "Every year, a couple hundred players retire, and baseball has only a few manager jobs, that's it. So, you see the problem."

"I see the problem, yeah, but I—"

"It's not the same as playing," cut in Paul. "You gotta know . . ."

"How to manage," Fritz finished.

"Exactly," agreed Paul. "You gotta know how to manage."

"I can learn."

Fritz rubbed his forehead. "Dexter, look. Managers spend years learning their craft. They start as scouts, then player personnel, then third-base coach, then bench coach. Then, just then, they get a shot at Double A and work their way up to Triple A before they can get to the show."

"You have a job opening in Scranton—"

"That's Triple A," blurted Paul. "Guys wait their whole lives to manage at that level."

"I can do it," insisted Archer. "if you give me a chance."

"Maybe you could be batting coach for the Sacramento River Cats," Andy said with a smile.

"Or first base coach for the Arizona Silver Ponies," said Paul, nodding.

"Or take tickets for the Frisco Rough Riders," said Fritz, and the guys burst out laughing.

Archer ignored them. "If you just give me a shot, I can—"

"I know you think you can manage—a lot of guys do," said Andy. "But it's not that easy."

Fritz jumped in. "Look, Dexter, you're rich, you're famous. The fans love you, so take it easy—go fishing, play golf—"

"I don't want to play golf," he responded.

"Then play shuffleboard for all we care," said Andy.

"You just can't . . .," said Fritz.

"What?" asked Archer.

"You just can't . . ."

"Manage?" asked Archer.

"No. Sorry," replied Fritz.

Archer looked around the table at each of them and saw the same thing in their faces—no. He rose without saying a word, turned his back to them, and walked to the door.

"Dexter," said Fritz, "come back."

But Archer did not turn around.

"Dexter, be reasonable," Fritz called after him. But Archer went out without another word and slammed the door behind him. Fritz turned to the other guys. "Well, somebody had to tell him," he said with a sigh, flopping down in his chair. "Somebody had to tell him."

Chapter Fourteen
DOGS DON'T PLAY BASEBALL

"Come on, there's a greasy spoon on the next block," said Eddie. He led Louie and Sally down the block to the diner on the corner. They entered and walked past the stools, with the short order cooks shouting from the kitchen, and slid into a booth in the back.

"You hungry?" said Eddie.

"Sure," said Sally. "I'm always hungry."

"Then order. It's on me," said Eddie.

The waitress came over, flipped her pad. She was a squat woman who walked with a slight limp, with her hair up and two pencils through the bun, in a thin white waitress uniform with a blue collar, and stubby fingers and a well-set jaw. She stared down at them like she was doing them a favor. "Whattaya gonna have?" she said.

Eddie ordered first. "I'll have a bagel with butter and cream cheese, French fries with ketchup, and two strips of bacon extra crispy."

"Bagel down with butter and a smear, red shoes walkin', and two oinkers extra leather," she yelled to the kitchen. She turned to the kids. "What'll youse guys have?"

"I'll have a tuna sandwich," said Louie.

"On?"

"Rye."

"Snappin' on rye," she yelled to the kitchen. She turned back. "And you?"

"I'll have a hamburger," said Sally.

"How do you want it?"

"Medium."

"Hockey puck pink," she yelled.

"And to drink?"

"A coke for me," said Louie. "Me, too," said Sally. "Coffee for me," said Eddie.

The waitress flipped her pad, went off, came back, and slung the cokes on the table, spilling the suds and the coffee. She nodded, *like there, you got it, don't you? So, give me a break.* And she wandered off to give somebody else a hard time.

"Okay, so we gotta find a manager, right?" said Eddie, sipping his coffee.

"Right," said Louie and Sally together.

"So, who we gonna get?"

"We don't know," said Louie.

"I'm not much of a baseball guy, so you got to help me out here."

"Uhhhhh . . .We don't know anyone," said Sally. "We're kids."

"Hmmm," said Eddie. They sat in silence for a while, thinking. The waitress returned with the food and threw the plates on the table.

"This bagel is burnt," said Eddie, looking up at the waitress.

"You don't like it, take it up with management," she said, walking off.

"Guess I'll eat it," said Eddie.

"I like her," said Sally.

"She reminds me of you," said Louie.

"Very funny."

Eddie started eating the bagel, talking between bites about managers and where to find one and what they'd say to them if they ever talked to one, when he looked up at the next table, and stopped eating. He squinted. Louie and Sally turned around to see what he was looking at. The man at the next table, an older guy in a windbreaker with curly hair combed back, was reading the *New York Post*. The back page, the sports page, had a big picture with a screaming headline.

"What's it say?" asked Eddie.

Louie read it out loud, "YANKS SAY NO WAY TO D. A."

"Who's D. A.?"

Sally and Louie turned around and stared at him, like, *you don't know D.A.?*

"Whaaaatt?" replied Eddie. "I told you, I'm not a baseball guy."

"D.A. is Dexter Archer, only the most famous shortstop to ever play for the Yankees," said Sally.

"And the best," added Louie.

"Yeah, sure, I heard of *him*."

"I would think so," Sally said.

"So, what's it mean?" asked Eddie.

"What's what mean?"

"The headline. YANKS SAY NO WAY TO D. A. What's it mean?"

"I don't know," said Sally, with a shrug.

Eddie got up and walked over to the man at the table. "Excuse me, could we get a look at your paper when you're done?" he asked.

"You want my paper?" he said gruffly. "You want my paper???"

"Yeah, I want your paper," replied Eddie. "When you're done."

"Sure, I'm done, take it," he said, pushing it towards Eddie.

"Thanks." He took it back to the table. The back cover of the paper had the giant photo of Dexter Archer, in his business suit, coming out of Yankee Stadium with an angry look on his face.

"What's it say?"

Louie read, "The Yankees SHUT THE DOOR on retired star shortstop Dexter Archer in his quest to become a manager, after giving him the heave-ho at a meeting yesterday at the stadium. The soon to be Hall of Famer reportedly asked the Yankee brass to give him a shot at managing Triple A. Yanks to Archer, "DROP DEAD.""

"He wants to manage?" asked Eddie eagerly. "He wants to be a manager?"

"Guess so," said Louie, nonchalantly.

Eddie stared right at them, then put his arms out in a gesture of *"Come on, don't you get it?"* Louie and Sally stared right back.

"Are you kidding?" said Sally.

"You want Dexter Archer to be our manager?" Louie asked in amazement.

"He's the most famous baseball player in the world," Sally said.

"Yeah, but he's out of a job now, it looks like," Eddie shot back.

"You're nuts," said Louie.

"No guts, no glory," said Eddie, getting up and throwing down a couple of twenties on the table.

In a huge two-floor apartment in a building not far from where they were having lunch, on the twenty-third floor, it just so happened that Dexter Archer was watching TV. Well, not exactly TV. He was sitting in his game room, with the walls filled with life-size photos of—Dexter Archer. He was surrounded by trophies big and small on the shelves, along with the bat that he used to get his last hit at Yankee Stadium, a walk-off game winning hit to right field. He wasn't wearing his business suit anymore. Now he was wearing an old Yankees tee-shirt, dirty jeans, no shoes. He was unshaven and his hair was a mess. On his big screen TV, he was watching a highlight reel of—himself, the great Dexter Archer, making great plays. The reel ended, so he pushed the button on the remote to go back to the beginning and play it again.

In the video, he made a great throw from shortstop, then turned a double play at second, then hit a line drive in the World Series, then caught a popup over his shoulder in left field. He was completely absorbed in the highlight reel when somewhere in the back of his mind he heard—a key in the door! He bolted up and off the couch, ran to the TV, frantically hit the eject button on the DVD player over and over, yanked the DVD out of the machine, and put it behind his back just as his wife Sarah walked into the room.

"Hi, honey," he said, his voice a bit higher than usual. He stood there, with the DVD behind his back, looking, well, guilty. She looked him over.

"Dexter," she said, "what have you been doing?"

"Nothing," he said.

"What's that?" She looked around behind his back.

"Nothing."

"Let me see—" And reaching around, she grabbed his arm and pulled it. There it was, the DVD: *Dexter Archer's Highlight Reel.* "Dexter!" she yelled, ripping the DVD out of his hands.

"What? I was just watching for a second," he said.

Her face softened, and she put her arms around him. "Dexter, what are we going to do with you?" she said sweetly. He hung his head. "Dexter, you can't just sit around here and watch your highlight reel. It's a little creepy, if you want to know the truth. And it's not good for you."

"I know," he conceded.

"You gotta find something to do."

"I went to the Yankees. They turned me down," he said.

"Then maybe there's something else you can do."

"That's all I want to do. I want to manage."

"Then find a team," she said, wandering off to put away the groceries. "And for God's sake, stop watching your highlight reel."

Andrea burst into the office, where Eddie, Sally, and Louie were lounging around, early in the morning, wondering what they were going to do about a manager. "Okay," she said, "I got it." It was three days later. They jumped up off the couch and gathered around. Andrea put down her Versace bag and spread out a map of New York City on the desk. "Okay, here we go," she said. "Dexter Archer lives on Seventy-third Street between Third and Lex, right here," and she pointed with her very manicured red nail to the street on the map where he lived. "He lives on the twenty-third floor. The doorman's name is Ray. He told me everything." She turned to Eddie—"I had to promise him a date, but don't worry, it'll be quick"—and then turned back to the map.

"You promised him a date?" said Eddie. She ignored him.

"His wife's name is Sarah, and she comes and goes all the time. Archer never leaves. He just sits around watching his highlight reel."

"Ohhhhh," they all said.

"Except—" They perked up. "Every morning at ten-thirty he comes out of the building and walks three blocks to here"—she pointed to a spot on Lexington Avenue—"Coffee Palace."

"He goes to Coffee Palace?" asked Sally.

"Every morning at ten-thirty. It's a ritual. Never misses a day. At least, so says Ray."

"The one you have a date with?" scowled Eddie.

"Anyway, so I wandered over to Coffee Palace and talked to the barista, cute little thing, and she said, yep, Dexter Archer comes in here every day around ten-thirty and orders a triple *venti*, half-sweet, nonfat double caramel *macchiato*, with two straws."

"Two straws?" said Sally.

"Yep, two straws. And if you leave right now, you can get there by ten-thirty and maybe see the great Dexter Archer himself."

Thirty minutes later, they arrived at the Coffee Palace on Lexington Avenue just after ten-thirty—Sally, Louie and Eddie, sitting in Andrea's Mercedes, watching the coffee shop.

"Okay, let's go," said Eddie.

"I don't know about this," hesitated Sally. He looked at them. Louie and Sally sighed and said, "Right, we know, no guts, no glory."

"Come on." They exited the car.

Sure enough, when they entered the store, Dexter Archer was standing in line, looking over the baked goods in the counter case. He wore his cap down low over his face, to keep from being hounded.

"That's him," said Louie.

"It's Dexter Archer," said Sally, total awe in her voice.

"Dexter Archer," said Louie, his jaw dropping.

"Yeah, let's go talk to him," said Eddie.

"Think we should?" said Louie.

"I don't know about this," said Sally.

Archer was still in good shape, maybe not as good as when he won his first World Series, but tall and lean. Louie had never seen him up close. The baristas behind the counter giggled when he came up.

"Hi, Dexter," said the cute barista, smiling perkily. "Still married?"

"Have to check," he said. He held up his wedding ring. "Yep, still married."

"I wasn't asking for me," said the girl shyly. "It's for the girls in the back." And the girls in the back started giggling uncontrollably.

"Triple *venti*, half-sweet, nonfat caramel *macchiato*?" she asked.

"Double caramel," he corrected. "With two straws."

"Right. Coming up." Archer swiped his credit card, pulled his cap down, and wandered over to wait for his coffee.

"Okay, now," said Eddie.

"Sure this is a good idea?" asked Louie.

"Come on." Eddie moved in. He walked right up to Dexter Archer.

"Mr. Archer," began Eddie.

"Sure," said Archer, "got a pen?"

"Huh?" It threw Eddie off for a moment, then he realized what Archer meant. "Oh, I don't want an autograph—"

"I do," Sally chimed in.

"So do I," said Louie.

"We want to talk to you about something else," said Eddie.

"Call my agent. Everything goes through him."

"Triple *venti*, half-sweet, nonfat double caramel *macchiato*," yelled the girl behind the counter, giggling. "For Dexter Archer!" All the customers swiveled their heads around and craned their necks to see him. He smiled, waved, picked up his drink—and headed for the door.

"We just need a minute," Eddie pleaded, in hot pursuit.

"Sorry, no time." Archer said, walking through the door to the street. Eddie stayed right with him, and Louie and Sally kept up behind Eddie.

"We have a proposition for you that we think you will like—" said Eddie.

"Sorry, gotta run," insisted Archer.

He was getting away up Lexington Avenue, and Eddie gave up and stopped, so Louie blurted out, "We have a team for you to manage."

Archer stopped, turned around, and said, "A team?"

"Yes, a team," said Louie.

"What kind of team?"

"We'll tell you," said Sally, "but you have to come with us."

"Is it a minor-league team?"

"Uhhhhh . . . kind of," said Louie.

Just then Andrea pulled up in her Mercedes and rolled down the window. "Hiya, Arch," she said, "Sit up front." So he got in. Louie, Eddie, and Sally crammed into the back as they drove up Madison Avenue, across the Harlem River Bridge, onto the Major Deegan Expressway, into the Bronx, past Yankee Stadium until they reached Van Cortland Park. They pulled up to an empty baseball diamond.

Archer got out and looked around. "Okay, I'm here. Where are they?" he said, looking at his watch impatiently.

"Oh, they'll be here," said Louie.

"Okay, I have an appointment, so I can't—"

Bursting from the dugout, the kids ran onto the field and started setting up bases.

"Little League?" asked Archer, scowling. "It's a Little League team?"

"Uh, not exactly . . .," said Louie.

A moment later, out of the dugout came the dogs: Bull the Bulldog, Oscar the German Shepherd, Pearl the Scotty, Chester, Marmalade, and all the others. The dogs ran onto the field and took their positions.

"There," said Louie. "There's your team."

Archer looked back at the field, where the dogs were warming up, then back at Louie, then back at the field, then back at Eddie and Sally, then back at the field.

"Where?" said Archer, genuinely confused.

"There." Sally pointed to the field.

"Mr. Archer," said Louie, taking a deep breath, "the dogs are your team."

Archer looked back at the field, then back to Eddie, then back at the dogs, then back at Louie and Sally, then back at the field, then back at them.

"The *dogs*?" he asked. "The *dogs* are my team?"

"Yes, sir."

"The dogs, those dogs, those dogs out there, are my team?"

"That's right," said Louie. "Those dogs play baseball—"

"You got me out here to manage a team made up of *dogs*?" said Archer.

"That's right."

"But you see, Mr. Archer," said Sally, "these dogs can actually play—"

"This is the craziest thing I've ever heard," said Archer, the veins popping in his neck.

"Well, if you actually watch, you'll see that—"

"This is crazy," Archer blurted, his face flushing red. "Absolutely crazy. I'm outta here." He started for the car.

"Dexter, wait," said Eddie. "Please."

Archer stopped and wheeled around. "Eddie, I've heard of a lot of dumb things in my time, but this may be the dumbest."

"But these dogs can actually play," replied Eddie. "Really."

Archer got right in his face. "Eddie, let me tell you something. Dogs don't play baseball. People do. Not dogs. People. You got that?"

"Well, usually that's true, I'll give you that, but in this case—"

Archer snapped. "Not dogs, people. People, Eddie. Not dogs. And certainly not those dogs. Now, get out of my way."

Eddie hesitated—then stepped aside to let Archer pass. Archer got back into the car with Andrea. "Let's go," he ordered. Andrea looked at Eddie, rolled her eyes, and hit the gas. The car skidded out of the parking lot, and they watched it go. Eddie sat down on the park bench and hung his head. Sally and Louie came over and sat down next to him.

"Don't worry, Mr. Antonetti," said Louie, "it'll be okay."

"You'll be our manager," said Sally.

And Eddie groaned, so loud that it might have been heard at Dodger Stadium in Los Angeles, California, far, far away.

"But I don't know how to manage," he said.

Chapter Fifteen
FRONT PAGE STORY

Saturday morning, just as the sun was drying the dew on the trees in front of his house, Louie came downstairs with Chester. From the breakfast table, his mother and father looked up.

"Big game today," said his dad.

"We're gonna get creamed," Louie said. "Creamed."

"Well, if you do, everyone's gonna see it," said Al. Louie looked confused, so Al pushed the *New York Post* across the table. Louie stepped forward to the table. And there, on the front page of the *Post*, larger than life, in flaming color, was a giant photo of—

"Chester!" yelled Louie. "Oh, my God, it's Chester, on the front page!"

"Yup," said his father. "Sure is. And look at the headline."

Louie read it aloud: "THE DOGS WHO PLAY BASEBALL. You're famous, boy." Chester wagged his tail. He looked at the story on the front page and muttered, "She did it."

"Did what?" asked his mom.

"She wrote the story."

"Who?"

"The reporter from the *Post*. She wrote the story after all."

"Well, now everyone knows," said his father.

"Everybody will be watching now," said his mother. "The whole city."

"Oh, noooooooo," wailed Louie, smiling in spite of himself. "Chester," he said, "you're a star."

Back at Archer's apartment, Sarah was returning from her morning run. "Here, I got you the paper," she said, throwing down a copy of the *New York Post* on the breakfast table, then going off to shower. Archer pushed the paper aside without even a glance as he ate his breakfast next to a cereal box with his picture on it. The back cover of the *Post* was face up, showing a giant photo of a big white Labrador, with a headline underneath: THE DOGS WHO PLAY BASEBALL. But Archer, his head down, didn't see it. He got up from the table, poured some more orange juice, then came back and sat down again and looked at his phone. He still didn't see the paper or the subhead: DOGS PLAY TODAY.

He put his orange juice glass right on top of the newspaper. He ate some toast. He picked up his orange juice glass again and took a sip and put it back. He took a last bite of toast, finished his cereal, then took his plate to the sink and poured some more coffee. Sarah came back into the kitchen, drying her hair with a towel, made herself some toast, and sat down at the table. "Hey, throw me the paper," she said. "I want to do the Jumbles."

Archer picked up the paper without looking at it and handed it to her.

"Look," she said, looking at the front page. "Isn't that cute?" She pointed at the giant photo of Chester.

"What is it?" said Archer.

She read the story quickly. "There's a baseball team made up of dogs."

"What?"

She read it to him.

NEW YORK, NY—The Bronx Bombers better watch out, because a group of kids in the Bronx have taught their dogs how to play baseball, really how to play baseball, and today the Bronx Barkers, as they are called, will play their first official game against a very good high school team, the Roosevelt Lions.

"They're sooooo cute," said Sarah, turning the page to reveal a team photo of all the dogs. Archer did a double-take.

"Let me see that," he said, ripping the paper from her hands.

Chapter Sixteen
NO BARKING IN BASEBALL

The stands at Teddy Roosevelt High School started filling up at noon for the big game. Signs went up in the stands: "WOOF THIS," "DOGS RULE," and "DOG DAY AFTERNOON."

The field was a well-manicured high-school field, with a metal fence in the outfield and cars parked beyond the fence, two cement dugouts with dirt floors, and grandstands behind home plate and up both first- and third-base sides. These grandstands were filling up. And the fences along the foul lines filled up as well. The grass was in good shape, better than anything Louie and Sally were used to, and the dirt in the infield had been swept smooth for a perfect ground-ball hop. Around one o'clock, the media started showing up, in TV trucks with satellite towers for live feeds with overdressed reporters putting on makeup in the shadow of the trucks. The crowd was already singing, "Take Me Out to the Ball Game," but they changed the words to, "Take me out to the Dog Park."

A banner hanging off the backstop read: LOUIE'S MOM GOT IT GOING ON. DONATE ONLINE FOR HER OPERATION. It was that very banner that Louie and his mom and dad saw as they drove up and turned into the parking lot in their white pickup a few minutes later.

"You're raising money for my operation?" asked his mother, with a concerned glance.

Louie nodded. Mimi squinted to read it. "So, what does that mean, *Louie's Mom's got it going on?*"

"It means they like you," fibbed Louie.

"Really? They don't even know me."

"It means they think you're hot," said her husband with a sly smile.

"Me?" she said, instantly flustered. "Well, if they say so . . ." and she beamed.

Louie got out of the pickup with Chester and ran over to join his team and the other dogs. The dogs ran in circles around them, getting their leashes all tangled up.

"Look, it's Mr. Park," yelled the kids. Mr. Park arrived with a giant bundle wrapped in brown paper.

"You need uniforms," he said, "Here." With that he opened the bundle and took out crisp white shirts and baseball pants, which he passed around. Sally held hers up. Emblazoned across the front it said, BRONX

BARKERS. "Team needs uniforms," said Mr. Park. The kids put them on.

"Whoa," they said.

"It's like being on the Yankees," said Sally.

"Go, Barkers." Mr. Park gave a cheer.

"Go, Barkers," yelled the team.

Two TV trucks, Channels 9 and 14, with their satellite dishes up in the air, did live updates from the field, the reporters in their ties and dresses, holding microphones.

"My," said Mimi, looking over the scene. "I hope this Mr. Antonetti knows what he's doing."

Cars filled the parking lot, and spectators exiting the subway poured over Van Cortland Avenue to the high school. By one o'clock the bleachers were full. And it was standing room only along the fence. Andrea's Mercedes pulled up and Eddie got out, wearing a Yankees cap and a dress shirt. Andrea looked over the crowd. "Look at all these people," she said. "More than coming to our wedding."

"One problem," said Eddie.

"What's that?"

"I don't know how to manage," he admitted.

"How hard can it be? Just bark at them," said Andrea, as she drove off to find a parking space.

Maggie Hart of the *Post* arrived in a taxi, waved at Eddie, and seated herself in the grandstand. She opened her pad. Eddie smiled and waved back.

From the door to the locker room, the high school team, the Roosevelt Lions, came running out onto the field and started warming up. They were older, almost like men, eighteen-year-old high-school players, tall, strong, some with beards or facial hair, and they threw the ball around like pros, whacking it deep into the outfield during batting practice. One batter sailed the ball over the center field fence.

"Uh-oh," said Sally.

"You can say that again."

Eddie stepped out of the dugout and surveyed his team, trying to at least look the part of manager.

"Skipper," said Sally, "you can't wear a dress shirt." She handed him his uniform.

Eddie put it on over his dress shirt. "Okay," he yelled, "let's bring it in." The kids and the dogs came running in and gathered around his feet. "Right, so we're going to have a good game, a tough game, and it'll be a game for the ages—" said Eddie. Sally snuck a look at Louie, like *do something*.

"Skipper," said Louie, cutting him off, "got a lineup card?"

"A lineup card?"

"Yeah," said Sally, "where's the lineup card?"

"What's a lineup card?" asked Eddie.

"Uh-oh," said Louie and Sally together.

They huddled with Eddie to draw up the lineup card. They put Donut the Mutt leading off, Oscar the

German Shepherd batting second, Bernie the Bernese Mountain Dog batting third, Chester the Labrador batting cleanup, Gabby the Bassett Hound batting fifth, Bull the Bulldog sixth, Pal the Great Dane in the seventh spot, Pearl the Scottie in eighth, and Marmalade the Whippet, the pitcher, batting last in the order.

"Okay," said Eddie, slipping the lineup card into his back pocket. "Let's play."

"Skipper," said Sally.

"Yeah?" said Eddie.

"You gotta give it to the umpire."

"Oh, right," he said and walked it out to the third-base umpire.

"Not him," yelled Louie, pointing over at the home-plate ump. "Him."

"This is going to be interesting," said Sally, raising her eyebrows.

Eddie found the home-plate umpire and handed him the card, then returned to the dugout. "Okay, let's play," he said, clapping his hands together. "Let's bat a hundred."

"I think you mean a thousand," said Sally.

"Right."

The game got underway. Donut came up first. She took two pitches and then swung on the third and hit a line drive into right field. A perfect hit. The dugout erupted in cheers. But Donut just stood at home plate and didn't move.

"Run, run," they yelled from the dugout.

"What's wrong with her?" said Eddie.

"I don't know," said Sally.

"Run, run," everyone kept yelling. Cara whistled the command to run to first. And Donut finally took off—but the wrong way. She ran up the third base line, over third and into left field.

"No, no, noooooooooooo," yelled Eddie. "Not that way."

All the dogs saw Donut run by and took off after her, running around in wide circles. The crowd thought it was hilarious and started chanting, "Dogs rule, dogs rule, dogs rule." The kids had to run out onto the field and bring the dogs back to the dugout.

"This is no way to play a baseball game," wailed Eddie. "Even I know that."

The right fielder threw the ball into the infield, and the second baseman threw it over to first, and the umpire called Donut out. "And that was such a good hit," said Eddie, sadly.

Oscar the German Shepherd came up next and struck out. "Come on, you're supposed to hit the ball," yelled Eddie as Oscar trudged slowly back to the dugout.

"Skipper, don't yell at him," said Sally. "He's a dog."

"Sorry," said Eddie. "I forgot."

Bernie the Bernese Mountain Dog came up next, batting in the third spot. He hit the first pitch into the gap in right center and took off for first base like a rocket. "Okay, okay, now we're talking," yelled Eddie over the crowd noise. Bernie rounded first and headed for second, but when he saw a kid in the crowd eating ice cream, he veered off and ran to the stands and the boy gave him a lick, then took a lick himself. The Lions player came over and tagged him out.

"What the—?" yelled Eddie. "He's not supposed to do that."

"I see you're getting the hang of this manager thing," said Sally.

The Barkers took the field, but the dogs didn't know where to play, so they clumped up around second base. The first Lions batter hit a ground ball to Pearl, and she made a fabulous play to spear it—

"There you go. There you go," yelled Eddie from the steps of the dugout.

But then instead of throwing it to first for the out, she took off into the outfield with the ball in her mouth, and all the dogs ran after her, and now the whole giant pack of dogs were running around the outfield.

"Oh, my God, it's like herding cats out there," said Eddie.

"Dogs," said Sally.

"What?"

"You said, herding cats."

"Yeah?" said Eddie.

"Well, technically, they're dogs," she said.

"So, you're actually herding dogs," agreed Louie.

"Right," said Eddie.

Oscar the German Shepherd came out of the game, walked up to Juan and put his head on his lap.

"Skipper, you got to take Oscar out," said Juan.

"Why?" said Eddie.

"He got some bad pizza."

"You gave him pizza?"

"Only two pieces."

The next Lions batter hit a home run and circled the bases and scored, so it was Lions 2-Barkers 0. The next batter hit a fly ball that Pal the Great Dane missed because he was eating cookies thrown to him from fans in the bleachers. Lions 3-Barkers 0.

The next batter walked. The next hit a double, and the player on first came all the way around to score. The score was Lions 4-Barkers 0.

"Uh-oh," said Sally.

"You can say that again."

Next batter hit a sky-high ball that Oscar, back in the game in right field, let drop and then picked it up and ran into the parking lot with it. Lions 5-Barkers 0.

"And it's only the first inning," moaned Eddie. He threw down his hat. "That's it," he yelled. "I've had it. I'm not doing this anymore. I'm done, done, done. I'm not a manager and I'm not not not going to do it."

At that very moment, a tall, lone figure entered the dugout, in a crisp white Yankees uniform, his cleats digging into the dirt, and his dark blue Yankee hat almost touching the top of the dugout. Louie looked up and his eyes widened. Sally looked up and her mouth fell open. All the kids looked up. Everyone stared. Sensing something, Eddie stopped flailing around and looked up. And there was Dexter Archer, the Yankee great.

"I got this," he said.

"Really?" said Eddie. *"Is it really you?"*

Archer nodded at him. "Okay, bring it in," said Archer, and the kids and dogs gathered around. "Okay, now we're gonna play some baseball." The dogs sat at attention and the kids nodded vigorously. "Here's the positions. The Labrador—"

"Chester," said Louie.

"Right, Chester's at first, the Scotty at second, the Mutt's at short, Bulldog's at third."

"Got it," said the kids happily.

"The German Shepherd's in left, the Great Dane stays in center, and the Collie goes in in right. Got it?"

"Got it," they said all together.

"The big guy—"

"Bernie!"

"He's behind the plate."

"Who's pitching?" said Sally.

"That's easy, the skinny one," said Archer.

"Marmalade."

"Okay, get out there and play some baseball," said Archer.

The kids jumped up and whistled to their dogs. The dogs jumped up, and the kids led the dogs out onto the field.

"And no doggin' it out there," yelled Archer. The kids stopped and turned. The dogs stopped in their tracks, and everyone turned and stared back at him.

"What?" said Archer. "What did I say?"

"Doggin' it?" said Sally. "Really?"

"Oh, Jeez, sorry. I'm sorry, okay? Now, get out there and play some baseball." The dogs turned around and ran to their positions.

The next Lions batter hit a ground ball to third. Bull came up with it, flipped it into the Fling Basket on his tail, whipped around, and fired to first for the out.

"Now, that's baseball," yelled Archer, clapping his hands. Then, quietly, he said, "Of course, it's a bunch of dogs, but it's still baseball."

"You can say that again," said Louie.

The next batter hit a screaming line drive down the right-field line, and Chester lunged for it, leaping high like only a dog can do, and caught it for the out. "Nice play," yelled Archer. "Give that dog a high five."

"How exactly do you do that, Skipper?" asked Sally.

"Not sure. It's never come up."

The inning ended, with the score still Lions 5-Barkers 0, and the dogs came up to bat. Pearl led off with a bunt, and ran like lightning to first.

"Saaaaaaaaaaaaaafffffe," yelled the ump, as her paw got there just before the throw.

"All right," yelled Archer. "We got something going."

Pal the Great Dane came up. Pearl took a lead off first. Bull the Bulldog came out onto the step of the dugout, tapped his nose with his paw, tugged on his ear, rotated his ears twice, and stuck out his tongue.

"What's he doing?" demanded Archer.

"He's giving signs," said Sally.

"Hey, I give the signs around here," Archer said. They pulled the Bulldog back into the dugout. Archer looked around and said quietly, "What was it?"

"Steal," said Sally.

"What's the sign for that?"

"Dog biscuit in the ear," said Louie.

"Figures."

Archer reached for a biscuit and put it against his ear. And on the next pitch, Pearl took off. The catcher fired it to second. The shortstop caught it and applied the tag to the sliding dog.

"Saaaaaaaaafffffe," yelled the ump, throwing his arms out in the safe sign, and the whole Barkers dugout went wild. Then Pearl sat down on the bag and would not get up.

"What's she want?" said Archer.

"A treat."

"This is baseball," said Archer. "There are no treats."

"Good luck with that," said Louie.

"She won't play unless she gets a treat," said Sally.

Archer looked out at Pearl sitting obstinately on the base. "Well, then, give her a treat."

"Time," yelled Sally. She ran out onto the field and gave Pearl a treat, and the dog popped up, ready to play.

"Nice job," said Archer. "Treats for everyone."

Marmalade, up next, hit a double, bringing Pearl around to score: Lions 5-Barkers 1. "Okay, we're on the board," said Archer. "The dogs are on the board." Then, after a moment, he said, "I can't believe I just said that."

Marmalade pitched a perfect second, third, and fourth inning. But the score didn't change, so it was still 5-1. The crowd settled in now, sensing that this now was a real game, that the Barkers had found their footing. A TV reporter went live in the sixth inning from the dugout, saying into the camera: *"After a rough first inning, this team of dogs, the Bronx Barkers, have settled down and allowed no runs. But the Lions still have a 5–1 edge going into the bottom of the sixth inning. And the amazing thing is, these dogs have shown everyone that they really can play baseball. Back to you."*

In the bottom of the sixth, Bernie the Bernese Mountain Dog came up and on the first pitch whacked a fly ball to deep right field, back, back, back and over the fence for a home run.

"Yes!!!" yelled Archer. The crowd went wild, chanting, "Bern-ie! Bern-ie!"

Chester barked. And all the other dogs started barking, too.

"Are you barking? Are you barking?" bellowed Archer. "There's no barking in baseball!"

The kids all groaned and rolled their eyes.

Champ the Collie came up and walked. Gabby the Bassett Hound came up and singled. Pearl the Scotty walked, loading the bases. And then up came Bull the Bulldog.

"Okay, Bull, show us what you got," said Archer.

Bull settled into the batter's box, digging in his feet for a good spin. He stared down the pitcher. The Lions pitcher threw a fastball, and Bull let it go by.

"Striiiiiiiiiike," yelled the ump.

The next pitch was a curveball, and Bull let that go by.

"Striiiiiiiiiike two," yelled the ump.

The next pitch came in fast and hard. Bull let it go.

"Ball," yelled the ump.

"Might have caught the corner," said Archer from the dugout. "It was close."

The next pitch was a fastball, and Bull turned, spun, and *whack*, hit a line drive into the gap in right field. Champ scored easily. Gabby scored. And Pearl rounded third and headed home for what would be the tying run. The throw came in. Pearl slid into home in a giant cloud of dirt. When the dirt cleared, the umpire had both his arms out flat.

"Saaaaaaaaaafffffe," he bellowed.

The entire Barkers bench went mad, yelling, jumping, screaming, throwing their arms around each other and the dogs. The scoreboard changed to 5-4.

"It's 5-4," yelled Sally, hugging Marmalade.

Donut the Mutt came up, his shaggy little body waddling to the plate, his hair sticking up all over, his tongue hanging out. He got set. The first pitch came in. He spun, he made contact, and the ball flew over third base and down the line. Donut easily got to second for a double. Bull scored to make it 5-5.

"We tied them," yelled Sally.

"Give that dog a treat," yelled Archer.

Pal the Great Dane came up, pawing the dirt around home plate. The crowd had now gone from laughing and joking to tense silence—on the edge of their seats. Pal took the first pitch, a strike.

"You can do it," yelled Chip, clasping his hands together as if in prayer. Pal let a pitch go by. "Strike two," yelled the umpire. Pal didn't seem to mind and stepped back in. The next pitch came in. Chip let out a howling whistle. Pal spun, the bat came up, and a little squibber came off his bat and rolled up the third base line.

The pitcher raced for it, but it got past him. The third baseman ran in, gloved it, and fired towards first. But Pal wasn't a Great Dane for nothing, and he flew— streaked—to first. He touched the bag *a second before* the ball got there. Donut rounded third and kept going for home.

"Noooooooo," yelled Archer. "Hold up." But the crowd was too loud. Donut couldn't hear. She was going to get home and get her treat, no matter what. The Lions first baseman, not expecting her to go for it, held the ball for a second before seeing Donut running. Then he threw the ball home. Cara whistled, and somehow Donut heard it over the crowd noise. She slid. The ball was thrown a little offline, to the first-base side, so the catcher had to reach for it, catch it, and then bring it back across his body for the tag. Donut slid. The catcher reached out his glove to apply the tag. Donut moved over to avoid the tag. She slid away from the tag and reached one little paw out and let it slide across home plate just as the catcher's mitt hit the paw.

"Saaaaaaaaaaaaaaaaaafe," yelled the ump. The stands rose and went absolutely nuts.

"Give that dog a treat," ordered Archer. "A big one."

The Barkers dugout all rose, hugging, high-fiving, shooting their arms in the air. Donut came waddling back towards the dugout, and Cara ran out and gave her not one but two dog biscuits. The scoreboard changed to Barkers 6—Lions 5.

"Okay, calm down, calm down," said Archer. "We gotta get through the last inning."

The Lions came up in the bottom of the ninth. "Three more outs," said Sally.

The first batter hit a line drive, and Donut made a circus catch at shortstop.

"Way to go, Donut," yelled Archer. "I never thought I'd say those words, but I just did."

"Two more outs," Sally quietly said.

The next batter hit a little grounder back to the mound, and Marmalade threw over to first for the easy out.

"One more out," said Sally.

Then, up came the best hitter on the Lions team, a tall, strong, lean, mean hitting machine. With facial hair, giant biceps, powerful legs, and the biggest bat Louie had ever seen, and he didn't look like a seventeen-year-old, but like a twenty-five-year-old major leaguer.

"Uh-oh," said Sally.

"Time," yelled Archer. He, Louie, and Sally all went out to confer with Marmalade. The four of them stood on the mound.

"Okay, can she throw a curveball?" asked Archer.

"No," said Sally.

"A slider?"

"No."

"How about a changeup?" said Archer.

"She's a dog, Skipper," said Sally.

"Okay, give her a treat and let's win this."

Sally gave Marmalade a treat, patted her on the head, and they went back to the dugout. Marmalade heard the whistle, wound up, and pitched. The batter let it go by. Ball one.

"You got this, Marmy," yelled Sally.

Marmalade threw another pitch, which the batter let go by. Ball two. Marmalade got the ball back, wound up, and threw a ball right down the middle of the plate. The batter swung. *Crack!* The ball flew high to center field. Coming off the bat, it almost surely looked like a home run.

But with the *crack* of the bat Pal the Great Dane was off. The ball started coming down, heading for the top of the outfield fence. Pal got a bead on it and made a giant leap, his head straining to get higher and higher and higher, over the top of the fence, and just as the ball was about to go over for a home run, Pal lunged and caught it.

The stands erupted. The dugout went crazy. The game was over.

"We won, we won, we won!" yelled Sally, hugging Louie.

The kids ran out on the field, past the stunned high schoolers—and hugged their dogs—then paraded them around the field. The Lions, being good sports, lined up, and the dogs lined up too, and the kids high-fived all the way down the line, with their dogs by their sides.

A TV reporter from Channel 6 went live in front of home plate. "Well, I guess dogs really can play baseball, as the Bronx Barkers have won their first game against a very good high-school baseball team, the Roosevelt Lions," the reporter said into the camera. "It's incredible, but these dogs fought back from down five runs to win six to five and claim the title best—the only, but still the best—dog team in the city."

Maggie Hart the reporter stood up in the stands and mumbled to herself, "The dogs who play baseball. Who woulda thunk it?"

On the field, Archer came out of the dugout and surveyed the chaos all around him.

"You won your first game as a manager," said Sally, coming up next to him with Louie.

"Congratulations," said Louie.

"Thanks," said Archer. "I guess."

"It's a start," said Sally.

"What do we do now?" said Archer.

Ice cream, that's what they did. Just like after every game, the kids and their dogs piled into the vans and station wagons and drove over to the ice cream parlor, where they ordered one cone each for the kids, and one each for the dogs. When Archer came in, everyone clapped and he smiled and waved. Pal the Great Dane got a big hand too for his game-winning catch. The dogs pranced around the ice cream parlor, licking their ice cream.

"Chocolate in a sugar cone," said Sally, ordering for Marmalade.

"Chocolate chip for Chester," said Louie.

The TV cameras came in and filmed the dogs eating ice cream. When Maggie Hart came in, everyone cheered and crowded around her.

"You wrote the story," said Louie.

"Well," said Maggie, "they're running my stories again, so yeah, why not?" She held up her phone for Eddie and everyone to see the *Post* headline from the online edition. The headline screamed: DOGS WIN! WOOF WOOF!

Eddie came rushing in, breathless. "Did you see?"

"See what?"

"We raised five thousand dollars for Louie's mother," he announced.

"Five thousand dollars?" said Louie. "That much?"

"Five thousand, two hundred and seventy-four dollars, to be exact—for your mom's operation."

"Wow," said Sally. "That's incredible."

"And think about what we'll make next time," said Eddie—and the room suddenly grew silent.

"What next time?" asked Archer.

"Listen to this," said Eddie, with a thrill in his voice. "I got us a game against the Brooklyn Cyclones." No one moved. No one said a word. No one even took a breath.

"Eddie, that's a Triple A team," said Archer.

"I know. Isn't it great? On for Saturday night."

Everyone turned to Archer—to see what he would do. He rubbed his chin, thought about it, weighed it, let out a long breath, looked up, and said, "Sure, why not?"

The place went crazy.

"Does this mean," asked Andrea when the noise died down, "that we gotta go to another game? Cause there's only so much baseball a girl can take."

Chapter Seventeen
SMILE ON A SUMMER EVE

A light tapping at the door woke Louie. Chester put his head up. Louie sat up and saw his father standing there.

"What?" he said.

"I thought you might want to help me with something," whispered his dad.

"What?"

"Come on," he said, "you'll see."

Louie and Chester made their way downstairs a few minutes later to the kitchen, where his father had toast and marmalade.

"Where's Mom?"

"She left early to visit Aunt Jenny. She won't be back till dinner. So, we have all day."

"For what?"

Al drove them in the pickup truck over to the hardware store, parking in the back of the lot. They jumped out and walked through the main entrance, with Chester tagging along. Al went right to the lumber aisle to pick out the wood. They filled the cart with two-by-fours, several sheets of plywood, nails, glue, and sandpaper.

"What's this for?" asked Louie.

"You'll see," said his dad.

At the counter, some teenage girls screamed, "It's Chester!" like groupies at a rock concert. Louie let the girls gather around and take selfies with Chester, who didn't seem to mind at all, and a crowd gathered to take photos and pet him. Al and Louie shook their heads. They got out of the store without too much more trouble and loaded the pickup truck.

"You're still OK riding in the back, aren't you, Chester, now that you're famous?" asked Al.

Chester jumped in and lay down on the lumber without so much as a bark. With the plywood sticking out the back of the truck bed they drove out on Bayside Avenue and were home in minutes. After unloading, they carried the stuff inside.

The next few hours were a blur of hammers, wood, cutting, nailing, measuring, and leveling until they were done. It took a bit longer than expected, and they were still putting away their tools when they heard the garage door opening. They heard the wheelchair lift in the garage, so they knew Mimi was home.

"Come on, quick," whispered his father, motioning them to slip out the back door into the yard. Chester followed.

A moment later Mimi rolled into the house. "Hello," she called out. "Anyone home?"

She wheeled herself into the kitchen, tossing the mail on the island. "Where is everybody?" she yelled. And then she slowly turned around because something was different in the kitchen. She wasn't sure at first what. Then she saw it.

Past the island, past the cabinets, past the sink and the dishwasher, on the other side of the room, a ramp, big enough for her wheelchair, now rose up to the window. She wheeled her chair over to the bottom of the ramp and looked it over, the smooth construction, the lovely railing, the perfect finish. With a few pushes, she rode her wheelchair to the top of the ramp, where she could look out the window into the backyard. Louie and his father were throwing the ball around.

"Hey, look, it's your mother at the window," said Louie's dad. "She can see us from there."

"Hi, Mom."

"You did this?" she said.

"Not us," said Al, "Chester did it all."

"So you could see us play baseball," said Louie.

Mimi wiped a tear from her eye.

Sally came over for dinner that night. They ate in the dining room, and Mimi made a feast: a roast, mashed potatoes, string beans, gravy, French bread. Al poured a little wine for Mimi and himself and served Sally and Louie a little grape juice in the good wine glasses.

"Looks wonderful," said Al, looking over the platters as they sat down.

"You always say that," said Mimi, smiling warmly.

"Because it always is *wonderful*," he responded.

"Oh, I forgot the bread," said Mimi, wheeling back.

"I'll get it." Louie jumped up and ran into the kitchen.

"You'll have to slice it," called his mother after him.

"Okay," he called back.

Mimi looked at Sally and smiled. "So, Sally, are you—?"

"Mrs. Cohen, Mr. Cohen," Sally cut in. "I just wanted to say that your son is amazing, I mean, really amazing. And, well, you already know that, but none of this would be happening without him, and I've never met anyone like him, never, and he's—"

Louie bounded back into the room just then, holding the breadbasket. They were all staring at him and he didn't know why.

"What?" he said, coming to a stop.

"I gotta go," said Sally, abruptly pushing back her chair out with a screech, and she ran out of the room. They heard the front door slam behind her. Louie looked at his parents, like, *what was that?*

"Just go after her, son," said his mother, softly. His dad nodded.

So, Louie went after her. He followed her out the front door into a perfect summer night. The trees were full, the light fading, the streetlights coming on, and there was quiet on the street. He looked around but didn't see her.

"Sally," he called. "Sally." No answer. "Sally."

"Over here," came a voice from the shadows. He found her sitting against a tree on the other side of the street. He walked over.

"You okay?"

She didn't speak. He sat down next to her, his back up against the tree. They sat in silence for a while, just the two of them and the pleasant evening.

"You know, Louie, you never told me," she said.

"Told you what?"

"What happened, you know, with your mom."

"Oh, that." Louie took a long time to answer. He had to reach back in his mind to that day long ago, that horrible day, and then put it all into words, something he had never tried to do before. "Well, we were driving back from Queens, and Mom was driving—"

"You were in the car?" blurted Sally.

"Yeah, I was—in the back seat."

"And?"

"Some guy ran a red light and hit us. On her side."

"Were you hurt?"

"I was okay because I was in the back, but . . ."

"She wasn't."

"No, she wasn't," said Louie. "She never walked again."

"That's awful." Sally's face was soft and glowing in the streetlight.

"I always thought, maybe I could have done something," he said.

"What could you have done? It was an accident."

He didn't answer, because deep down he wasn't sure.

"You know," said Sally, looking out into the fading summer light, "everybody thinks that because I don't wear dresses and I play baseball, and I don't wear makeup, that—"

Louie leaned over and kissed her. He wasn't quite sure how to do it, and at first it didn't go well, his nose hit her nose, but then he got it right and it was a good kiss. When he broke it off and looked at her in the streetlight, he could see her smile, like maybe the biggest smile ever.

"You hungry?" he said.

She nodded, still beaming.

"Wanna go in?"

She nodded, more vigorously this time. Back in the house, back in the dining room, they saw Al playing with a bobblehead toy on the table, but it wasn't Dexter Archer or Mariano Rivera, it was—

"Chester!" exclaimed Sally, her mouth dropping open. "A Chester bobblehead doll."

"Where did you get this?" asked Louie.

"They're selling them outside the subway," said Al, who gave it a little flick with his finger, and Chester's head bobbled.

"Chester, you're really famous now, like Dexter Archer," said Louie.

Chester barked.

"Are you barking?" said Louie. "Are you barking?"

They all joined in. "'Cause there's no barking in baseball!"

Chapter Eighteen
THE RING

All by herself, seated at her desk at the office, Andrea was talking to herself.

"Oh, my God, it's too much! Too much! Look at all these media requests. Good Morning America. CBS Sunday Morning. Fox News Sunday. I gotta deal with all this, and where's Eddie? He's out at a photo shoot for dogs, that's where he is."

She shuffled through the hundreds of requests for interviews, photos, TV appearances. She looked over at her computer, where she had over six hundred emails, all asking questions like, *"Is Chester available for an interview?"* or *"What do the dogs eat before a game?"* or *"Is Marmalade a hologram?"* A sneaker company was offering Oscar an endorsement deal, and Wheaties wanted to put Bull the Bulldog on the front of their cereal box.

"I can't do all this," wailed Andrea. "It's too much."

Her job was not just to handle the media, but with the big game coming up, the other arrangements fell to Andrea as well—stocking the locker room with dog biscuits, getting photos of the dogs to the networks, sending the uniforms to the laundry, basically everything. "I liked it better when we had nothing to do," she sighed. "And all because of a bunch of dogs!"

She wrote a few replies to the emails, answering, "No, Marmalade is not a hologram," and "The dogs do not have a movie deal yet," when a knock came at the door. She got up and opened it and there was the building agent, holding a white envelope.

"You're out," he snapped.

"We're what?"

"You haven't paid your rent," said the building agent. "You're out."

"Out of where?" said Andrea, trying to stay calm.

"Out of this office. This is your eviction notice." He held out the envelope again.

"Now, be reasonable," said Andrea.

"I want you out of here by the end of business today," he said firmly.

"Please," she pleaded. "We can pay the rent. We just need—"

At exactly that moment, pushing aside the building agent, who should waltz in but Eddie Antonetti, carrying several boxes and bags from the department store, the computer store, and the famous store with the little blue boxes.

"Eddie, you're here!" Andrea motioned with her eyes towards the building agent. "He's from the building, you know, the building . . ." She made a little nod with her head, like *get it?*

Eddie turned to him. "Hello, good to see you," he said. Then he turned back to Andrea. "I have something for you."

"Maybe later," she said, in that *not now* kind of way. But Eddie would not be put off.

"Look what I have." He pulled a pair of high heels out of the bag. "Those Jimmy Choos you wanted. Now, I know you wanted them, so don't lie."

"Maybe we should do this later, Eddie? Like *later...*"

"And that laptop you wanted," said Eddie, pulling it out of the bag. "Huh? Huh? Pretty nice."

"Yes, Eddie, I see you've been a busy man, but—"

"Oh, and here you go," Eddie handed her the little blue box with a white ribbon around it. "It's from you know where."

"Yes, I can see that," said Andrea.

"Go ahead. Open it. Open it."

Andrea hesitated, looked at the building agent, then shrugged and opened it. Immediately her heart melted. It was dazzling. It was spectacular. It was a marvelous, giant, shiny, wonderful diamond ring, big as a house, and just the one she wanted. "Oh, Eddie," she gasped.

"Mr. Antonetti," the building agent cut in harshly.

"That's me," said Eddie, pointing. "Name's on the door, Eddie Antonetti, that's me."

"Yes, I can see that," he responded. "What I can't see is why you are buying all these expensive gifts when you can't even pay your rent."

"Rent?" said Eddie. "Did you say rent?"

"You haven't paid your rent in six months, so you're being evicted."

"Really?" said Eddie. "That's interesting, because…" Eddie pulled a bunch of envelopes from his jacket pocket and held them up and said, "Look what I have here—a rent check." He handed it to the agent. "For this month." He handed him another. "For last month." He handed him another. "For the month before that." And then he pushed all the checks at him in a bundle. "And here you go for the last six months."

The building agent stood there, sputtering. "This is…wonderful," he said.

"And here's a check," said Eddie, handing him one last envelope, "for the next six months."

"You're paying . . .?"

"In advance, I always pay in advance," said Eddie. "And I'll take that." Eddie reached over, plucked the eviction notice from his hand, ripped it in half, then half again, then half again.

"Yes, do that," said the building agent. "We won't be needing *that* anymore."

"Now, if you'll excuse us," said Eddie, walking him to the door. "We have a lot of work to do."

"Yes, of course, sorry for the inconvenience," stammered the agent. "I'll be going. Sorry to disturb you."

"Goodbye," said Eddie, pushing him gently out the door.

"And, Mr. Antonetti, I just want you to know if you need anything, anything at all, you just call down to my office and I'll be right up."

"That's nice," said Andrea, closing the door and crushing his fingers.

"Owwwww . . . ," he wailed from the hallway.

"Sorry," called Andrea through the door.

Eddie looked at her and went to kiss her. She put up her hand and opened the little blue box and held it out to him. "What?" he said. She nodded at the ring.

"But we're already engaged," he protested.

"Yes, but now you have the ring, so . . ." She nodded and her eyes said, *one knee, buster.*

"You gotta be kidding," he said.

"Go ahead, if you know what's good for you."

"Okay," he said, clearing his throat. "Andrea Spartarelli—"

"The knee."

"The knee?"

"The knee," she said.

"Do we have to –"

"Isn't that what you do when you give a girl a ring?" He rolled his eyes. "Don't roll your eyes at me, or maybe I won't say yes," she said.

"My luck!"

"Very funny."

So—he got down on one knee.

"That's good," she said. "Now go ahead."

"Andrea Spartarelli," he said, "since no one would ever be able to put up with you but me—"

"Do it right, Eddie," she demanded.

"Will you marry me, Andrea Spartarelli, and make me the happiest man alive?"

"Guess I have to," she said, "if I want to keep the ring."

He rose and slipped it onto her finger. She held it up to the light and the diamond glittered.

"You did good, Eddie Antonetti. I think I'll marry you, after all, even if you do hang out with a bunch of *dogs*."

Chapter Nineteen
FLOWERS EVERYWHERE

Flowers were everywhere. Everywhere! All over the office, by the window, on the desk, filling up the couch, just everywhere. Red roses. Yellow roses. White roses. Lilies, carnations, purple flowers, pink flowers, yellow flowers—every kind of flower you could think of—all piling up around Maggie Hart, the most talked-about reporter in the city, in her fancy new office at the *Post* on the tenth floor, right next to the editor's office, with a huge window overlooking the Hudson River. She had feet up on her massive new desk while talking on the phone with Eddie, as workmen moved all her new furniture in—couches, chairs, side tables, coffee tables, throw pillows.

"I got throw pillows, Eddie," she said. *"They gave me throw pillows!"*

"What's a throw pillow?"

"Not sure, but I got 'em."

"New office, huh?"

"Yeah, overlooking the river." She gazed around. A delivery man came in carrying a bouquet. "No more flowers," she yelled to him. "Give them to the girls downstairs."

"You're getting flowers?" asked Eddie.

"And I had three marriage proposals already this morning," she said. "Two from Jersey and one from Japan."

"Japan, huh?"

The editor-in-chief, Maximilian Morgan-Stewart, came sweeping into her office as the workmen set down her new sofa. Maximilian, who everyone called "Max Makes Millions," because of his $2,000 suits, took a seat on the couch. Maggie looked up and couldn't help but notice his shiny black Italian shoes, dazzling silk pocket square, striped shirt and well-coiffed hair.

"Gotta go, Eddie," said Maggie. "Talk later." She hung up. And as soon as she did, Maximilian immediately started talking, rapid fire, like a million words a minute.

"Hey, Mag, hi. Like the office? Good. Good. You can see the river, right? See it? It's right there, see it? Good—good office, right? Keep writing those stories and you can keep it, okay? Okay, okay—here's the deal. Here it is. Ready? You ready? People love the dogs. The dog stories. They love them. LOVE THEM. You got that? L-O-V-E them. Circulation is up thirty percent since you started writing about those stupid dogs. Thirty percent! You got that? Now, I know you want the Yankees back. Sorry, I can't help you there, not yet. But you can get them back, get back the New York Yankees, if you just keep these stories coming, keep 'em coming. Just get me more dog stories. Exclusives. They gotta be exclusives. Got that? Got it? That's it. I need more dogs. MORE DOGS! Do you get what I'm saying, Mag? Do you?"

Maggie nodded.

"Good." And with that, he stood up and started for the door. "Nice flowers," he said on the way out the door, looking over the wall of flowers. "Nobody ever sends me flowers."

Louie stepped back and looked up at the giant thermometer he had just finished drawing on poster board in his bedroom. It was three feet tall. He had drawn it with magic markers, red and black. He had drawn a big ball at the bottom, then a long stem going up to the top of the thermometer. He wrote $540,000 at the top. With his magic marker, he stepped forward and finished filling in a small amount of color at the bottom of the thermometer, then to one side wrote $5,240 next to the line. He looked back up at the top of the thermometer.

"Oh," sighed Louie. He wasn't quite sure how he was going to get all that money. "What do you think, boy? We got a long way to go, don't we?" Chester wagged his tail like crazy. "Don't worry, boy. We'll get there," he said. "Only five hundred thirty-four thousand seven hundred and sixty dollars to go."

From his closet, Louie took out his crisp white Bronx Barkers uniform, and laid it on the bed. He put on the pants first and tightened the red belt. Then he put on the jersey with "Bronx Barkers" written in baseball script across the chest. With one hand, he grabbed his hat and with the other his cleats to carry outside, since he wasn't allowed to wear them in the house.

"Louie, time to go," yelled his father from downstairs. Chester wagged his tail.

"Okay, boy, let's go play some baseball," said Louie.

Chapter Twenty
GET YOUR HOT DOGS

"Get your HOT DOGS," yelled the curly-haired vendor, making his way through the stands. "Right here, get 'em while they're hot. HOT DOOOOOOOGS." His voice echoed throughout the ballpark. Eddie, sitting twenty rows back, raised his hand. "How many?" yelled the vendor. Eddie raised two fingers. "Two coming atchya." The vendor threw two hot dogs wrapped in silver foil, one at a time, over twenty rows and hit Eddie right in the hands both times. Then he threw a tennis ball with a slot cut into it. Eddie slipped four bucks into the slot and threw it back.

"Get your hot dogs," yelled the vendor, moving on. "Hot dooooogs."

"Did you get the mustard?" said Andrea.

Coney Island, that's where they were. At the stadium of the Brooklyn Cyclones, the Triple A team affiliated with that *other* New York ball club, the New York Mets. Triple A is one step from the major leagues—and so the players going against the Bronx Barkers on this night were among the best in the game, only one step away from teams like the Yankees or the Dodgers, or the Phillies or the Twins.

Screams floated through the night air into the stadium from riders on the Cyclone, the roller coaster right next to the stadium. The Cyclones got their name from the historic New York amusement park ride, one of the most exciting rides in the whole country—the Coney Island Cyclone, an old-fashioned wooden roller coaster, which the fans could now hear rushing down from the grand height of eighty-five feet at sixty miles per hour.

"Get your PEANUTS," yelled another vendor, a bald guy with stubby fingers.

"You want peanuts?" Eddie asked Andrea.

"Of course I want peanuts."

"Two over here," yelled Eddie.

And the game was on—the Bronx Barkers against the Brooklyn Cyclones—on a perfect summer night, the waves crashing on the Coney Island Beach just a stone's throw away and the capacity crowd cheering them on, the Brooklyn Cyclones against a bunch of dogs.

The dogs were losing. It was Cyclones 5-Barkers 4 going into the ninth inning. The Bronx Barkers had one more chance to tie it up. Their *last chance*. Chester came up, waited on a fastball, and doubled into the right-field corner, easily beating the throw with a perfect slide into second.

Louie said quietly to Archer, "Send him."

"No way. He's on second."

"He'll beat the throw."

Archer sighed deeply and gave the sign. On the next pitch Chester took off, his paws digging into the infield, the dirt flying. He ran like a dart aimed at the bull's-eye at third base. From the edge of the dugout, Louie let out a low whistle and Chester slid headfirst into the bag, stretching out his paw and touching the base just before the tag.

"Saaaaaaaaaaaaaaaaaafe," yelled the third-base ump, throwing his arms out flat.

Archer took a deep breath. "Boy, that was close."

"Told you," said Louie.

Oscar the German Shepherd came up and on the second pitch hit a high fly to center. The center fielder, getting under it, made the grab. Chester tagged third and took off for home. The throw came in, but Chester beat it by a mile, tying the score: Cyclones 5-Barkers 5. Pearl beat out a bunt, Bull singled, Bernie hit a bloop fly that dropped in for a single, and Pearl, running on contact, scored from second. Now, the dogs had the lead, Barkers 6-Cyclones 5. And the stadium suddenly got very quiet, because the fans liked the dogs but didn't want to see them *actually beat* the Cyclones. Losing to a bunch of dogs was, well, like losing to a bunch of dogs.

So, the Cyclones came up in the bottom of the ninth down by one run, and the first batter hit a fly ball to right. Champ the Collie heard the whistle from Levar, got under it, and caught it for the out. One away. And that was about all the Cyclones' manager could take. He charged onto the field and right up to the home plate umpire.

"Those kids got to get off the field," demanded the manager.

"What are you talking about?" yelled back Archer, rushing up to home plate.

"The rule book says no players on the field unless they're up at bat, on base, or in the on-deck circle," said the manager. "And all of those kids are on the field."

"Oh, that," replied Archer, with a forced chuckle. "That's easy. The dogs need to hear them whistle. That's why they're out there."

"Rule's a rule. No one on the field during play," insisted the manager.

"But if the dogs can't hear the whistles—"

"Rule's a rule."

"But –"

"Are you going to go by the rule book or not?" the manager demanded of the ump.

The ump screwed up his face. He'd never had to make this kind of decision before. But he was clearly considering it now.

"Oh, you can't be serious—" sputtered Archer.

"Okay, rule's a rule," the ump ordered. "Get 'em off the field."

"You can't do that!"

"Off!"

Archer put his nose right in the ump's face. "Come on! No way!"

The umpire said in Archer's ear, "Dexter, you're my favorite player of all time, but if you don't get those kids off the field, I'm calling the game for the Cyclones."

"You can't do that," sputtered Archer.

"Try me," the ump said and turned his back to him.

Archer fumed, then stormed away back to the dugout. "Okay, back inside," he said to the kids outside the dugout.

"But Skipper, they can't hear our whistles from in there."

"Just get back."

Slowly, shaking their heads, the kids all moved back into the dugout.

The next Cyclones batter took two strikes and then hit a lazy fly ball to center field. Ordinarily, Pal the Great Dane would have made the catch easily. Chip whistled and whistled again and whistled a third time. But Pal didn't hear it and didn't know what to do. Falling on the grass, the ball rolled away. Pal wandered off in search of some popcorn from the stands, and the runner came around to score.

"Uh-oh," said Sally.

"You can say that again," said Louie.

The Barkers lost 7–6 in the bottom of the ninth. Game over.

Gathering his team up, Louie headed to the ice cream parlor on the boardwalk. They got their cones, but no one ate much, and the cones started dripping all over the place. The dogs ate theirs, though, and seemed to enjoy the ice cream as usual.

Louie and Sally walked along the boardwalk, with Louie lost in thought.

"We almost won," said Sally after a while.

"So?"

"That means something."

"Yeah, like what?"

"I see your point," said Sally.

"No one is ever going to play us again," said Louie. "We're toast."

"Maybe, or maybe not," said a voice. They turned and saw Archer, holding his phone displaying the *New York Post* website. The headline read, DEY WAZ ROBBED, with a photo of Bull the Bulldog and Donut the Mutt.

"We were robbed," said Sally.

"Yes, but next time, maybe we won't be."

"Next time?" asked Sally.

"What next time?" said Louie.

Dexter Archer's eyes twinkled, as he looked out over the Boardwalk at the crashing waves.

Chapter Twenty-One
DOGS AND BASEBALL

Next day, Archer's red Ferrari pulled up to Yankee Stadium under the hot summer's sun. The asphalt practically melted under the wheels of the sports car. Archer popped out, fixed his tie in the side mirror, smoothed his suit jacket, and adjusted his baseball cap. Then Sally got out, wearing a pretty dress, yanking it this way and that.

"I hate this thing," she sneered.

"I think you look good," said Archer. "Doesn't she look good?"

Louie, popping out of the Ferrari, looked over and said awkwardly, "Yeah, you do."

"Oh, brother," she said, pulling on the dress.

"Okay, let's do this," said Archer, leading them towards the stadium gate.

"Wait," said Louie. He held the door open for Chester and Marmalade to jump out. Bull the Bulldog, too.

"I almost forgot," said Archer. Then he shook his head. "They're gonna think I'm off my rocker."

"You *are* off your rocker," said Sally.

The workmen saw them and called out. Archer waved back, but then realized they were yelling for Chester. "Oh, brother," he said.

They walked through the gates into the stadium, eerily quiet now, the vendor booths locked up, the food concessions closed, the ramps empty. The elevator took them to the top floor, to the corporate offices, where they got out, with the dogs following close behind.

"Can I help you?" said a middle-aged secretary.

"Yes, I'm Dexter Archer—"

"You certainly are," she said, smiling.

"We're here to see the general manager."

She picked up the phone. "Mr. Archer is here to see you, with some of his furry friends," she said, nodding as she listened. "All right, I'll tell him." She hung up and turned to Archer. "He says to make yourself comfortable, he'll be right with you."

"Thanks very much."

"Sooooo cute," she said, looking over at the dogs. "Is that really Chester?"

Sally and Louie wandered around the office. On the walls were life-size posters of great Yankee players. They went from poster to poster, staring up at them. They stopped at a giant picture of Babe Ruth. "Wow," said Louie. "Wow," said Sally. They walked over to

Mickey Mantle. "Wow," said Sally. "Wow," said Louie. They stopped at Mariano Rivera's lifesize photo. "Wow," they said together. They stopped in front of the giant photo of Dexter Archer, an action shot. Archer walked up behind them as they looked up at the photo.

"Who's he?" said Sally.

"Never heard of him," said Louie.

"I wonder how *he* got up there."

"Very funny," said Archer.

"They're ready for you now," announced the secretary. As she ushered them through the lobby, the dog leashes got wrapped around the coffee table. It flipped over and Archer rolled his eyes. "Sorry," said Sally, freeing the dogs and setting the table upright. "Sorry."

The General Manager Fritz, along with his sidekicks Andy and Paul—the Yankee brass—stood up as they entered the conference room, all smiles.

"Hello, hello, come in, come in," said Fritz, as Archer, Louie, Sally, and the dogs entered. "And we have some dogs, I see."

"That's Chester. That's Marmalade. And that's Bull."

"Very nice to meet your dogs. And who might you be?"

"Louie Cohen."

"Louie Cohen, good baseball name," said Andy.

"And I'm Sally Cartwright. I play on the team with Louie."

"Can you hit the curveball?" asked Fritz, with a hint of sarcasm.

"Well, as a matter of fact, I can," said Sally matter-of-factly.

"Sign her. Sign her right away," called out Fritz to his guys, who laughed. He shook hands with them all. "Well, why don't we sit down, and you can tell us why you're here."

So, they sat down, with Archer, Louie, and Sally on one side of the table, with Marmalade, Chester, and Bull next to them, and Fritz, Paul, and Andy on the other side of the large conference table.

"I hear you found a team to manage," said Fritz, smiling at Archer.

"I have," he replied.

"And we hear you've been to the dentist," said Andy.

"The dentist?" said Archer, cocking his head in confusion.

"Yeah, 'cause you have so many *canines*," said Paul. There was the briefest of pauses, and then the three of them burst out laughing. "Get it, canines? Dogs? Canines?"

Archer sat stone-faced, as did Louie and Sally.

"Sorry," said Fritz, holding back his laugh, "but you gotta admit, it's funny."

"Yeah, putting together a team of dogs on the field must be kinda *ruff*," said Paul, and the guys split a gut again.

"People must think you're *barking mad*," said Andy, and the three guys doubled over again in a fit of laughter. Louie, Sally, and Archer just stared at them. Even the dogs stared at them, cocking their heads from side to side.

Fritz got a hold of himself. "Okay, okay, sorry about that, but you gotta admit—oh, forget it . . . All right, what can we do for you? Tell us why you're here."

"We're here about a game," said Archer, leaning forward.

"A game?" asked Fritz, furrowing his brow.

"What kind of game?" said Andy.

"A game between the New York Yankees and"—he paused and took a deep breath—"between the New York Yankees and the Bronx Barkers."

"You mean them?" said Fritz, looking at the dogs running around his office. "The *dogs*?"

"Yes." There was silence for a moment but their faces said it all.

"You can't be serious," said Andy.

"You want the Yankees to play a game against a bunch of mutts?" sneered Paul.

"Hear me out," Archer continued. "The All-Star Game is being played here in two weeks."

"Yep, two weeks from tomorrow," said Fritz. "The All-Star Game right here at Yankee Stadium."

"Here's our idea. We play a game, the Yankees against the Barkers."

"Here at the stadium?" asked Andy.

"Yes," said Archer. "Before the All-Star Game."

"For charity," Louie chimed in.

"Right," said Archer. "For charity."

"We're raising money for spinal-cord injuries," said Sally. "You see, Louie's mother needs—"

"Let's get serious," Fritz cut her off. "Look, you can't expect the New York Yankees, a major league team, to play a game against a bunch of silly dogs."

"They aren't silly," Sally whipped back.

"Sorry. No offense meant."

Archer tried again. "Look, think about this for a minute. The whole country will be watching, millions of people, and the goodwill will be incredible, and the Yankees will be raising money for a good cause."

"Arch, be serious," said Andy. "It can never happen."

"Why not?" demanded Archer. The room went quiet, and the Yankee brass just stared back. Louie broke the ice.

"Sir?"

"Yes," said Fritz, trying to sound friendly.

"There are two things that people like, dogs and—"

"Baseball," said Sally.

"Right," agreed Louie. "Dogs and baseball. And you'll have both."

Fritz smirked, crossed his arms and sat back in his chair. "Look, I know you mean well, and I wish you all the luck in the world, but we just can't do it. Sorry."

"Is that your final answer?" said Archer.

"I'm afraid it is."

"Well, we understand. We really do," said Sally.

"But *they* may not," said Louie.

"Who?" asked Fritz.

"Them." Archer got up and walked over to the conference-room door and flung it open. The first person to rush in was Eddie, followed by a gang of reporters and TV cameras. The reporters pressed against the table as the cameras got set up, shouting questions.

"What the—?" sputtered Fritz. "You can't—"

"Come in, come in," Archer said to the press, as they crowded around. "Make yourself comfortable. We'll have an announcement to make." He motioned to Louie and Sally to step up to the microphones. They rose.

"I'm Louie Cohen," he said into the microphone.

"And I'm Sally Cartwright."

"And who are you?" someone yelled at Archer. And that got a laugh from the reporters. But not from the Yankee brass.

Louie cleared his throat. "We'd like to announce that we have met with the Yankees front office—"

"And asked them to play a game against the Bronx Barkers—" continued Sally.

"And they have given their answer," said Archer.

Louie continued, "And their answer is—"

Fritz jumped up from his chair and cut in front of them, grabbed the microphone and said, "—that the New York Yankees will be playing a charity game against the Bronx Barkers before the All-Star Game two weeks from today."

The place went crazy. The reporters shouted questions, the dogs jumped on the chairs, and the cameras filmed the whole wild scene.

"OMG, we're really playing the Yankees," said Louie, looking on.

"Who woulda thunk it?" said Sally.

Chapter Twenty-Two
THE PRESS CONFERENCE

Game back on. Bronx Barkers to play bronx bombers! screamed the headline in the *Post*.

And just as Eddie had predicted, the Bronx Barkers were now famous all over the city. Everywhere they went, people went mad for them. They wanted to pet the dogs, take selfies, hug them, be seen with them, post pictures of them. In short, they were the toast of the city. Everyone wanted to feed them and brought dog treats, until Archer said, "No more. They'll get fat. They got a game to play." Mr. Park raised a banner over his store that read, HOME OF THE BARKERS, and his business went up 50 percent in one day. Everyone loved the Bronx Barkers.

Maggie Hart wrote stories in the paper, one story each day, front page stories about the dogs—what they ate, where they lived, what position they played, where they liked to be scratched. The morning TV shows wanted interviews, but Louie and Sally said no, only

Maggie got interviews. Everywhere on social media were photos of the dogs playing baseball, hitting, making spectacular catches, pitching, and the photos got lots and lots of likes. The New York City mayor held a ceremony at City Hall and gave them the key to the city. Donut tried to eat it, but then spit it out because it didn't taste very good.

The governor released a proclamation from the Capitol in Albany: "Be it proclaimed to the State of New York and the world, that July 9 is to be Bronx Barker Day." TV, radio, bloggers, magazines, newspapers—they all wanted a piece of the dogs who played baseball. Until it got to be too much. "Enough," said Archer. "Time to practice." So, they went down to Van Cortland Park and spent the day fielding grounders, catching fly balls, whipping the ball around, and taking batting practice. The dogs had never looked so good. At the end of practice Archer called them all together, kids and dogs.

"I've been to see the bosses at Major League Baseball," he said. "I asked them if you guys could sit on the field so the dogs could hear the whistles."

"Yeah," said Ron, "and what did they say?"

"They said no."

"Ohhhhhhhh," groaned the kids.

"But, Skipper, if the dogs can't hear the whistles, they won't know what to do," said Cara.

"They won't catch," said Donna.

"They won't hit," said Juan.

"They won't run," said Levar.

"We'll get wiped out," said Chip. And with that, everyone started jabbering loudly at once, so nobody could hear anything.

"Okay, okay," said Archer, "settle down. I'm not giving up, you know."

"You're not?" said Juan.

He turned towards the parking lot and yelled, "Okay, Al."

Al got out of his pickup. Al lifted several big boxes from the truck and set them down on the field. The kids gathered around as he unpacked them, opening them one by one and taking out the equipment.

"These are loudspeakers," he said, pointing to four huge speakers.

"Speakers?" said the kids.

"How will they work?" asked Levar.

Al started attaching the wires. "We'll set them up, and they can broadcast loud enough for the dogs to hear all over the stadium."

"Whoooooooa," they said.

"How do we talk into them?" said Ron.

"With this." Al held up a microphone.

"Whooooooooa."

"Where do we set it up?" asked Cara.

"At the top of the dugout," said Al. "Let's try it."

So, they set up the four speakers facing the field. Al plugged in the microphone and handed it to Donna, who looked at it funny.

"Try it," he urged.

Donna, without thinking, took a huge breath and whistled into the microphone. It came out so loud that everyone grabbed their ears and yelled, "Stop!"

"They could hear that at the Empire State Building," said Sally, taking her hands down.

They put Pal the Great Dane in center field, and while the kids screamed their heads off and made as much noise as they could, Louie hit a fly ball and Chip whistled into the microphone. Pal heard it, caught the ball, and whipped it back in.

"Who knew," said Sally. "A sound system."

"Let me try it," said Levar.

Everyone yelled at the top of their lungs, and Levar whistled over the racket. Champ the Collie caught a fly ball and threw it to second.

"Let me try," said Veronica. When she whistled over the din, Gabby the Bassett Hound slid into second.

"Let me try," said Chuck, and as he whistled into the microphone, Bull the Bulldog fielded a grounder at third and threw to first for an easy out.

"It works," said Louie.

They practiced all afternoon till the dogs could follow all the whistles from the loudspeakers. By the end of practice, they had it down.

"Okay," said Archer, calling them all together, "keep practicing your whistles so your dogs will know them all by game time."

"Okay, Skipper," said the kids.

Just then some tires screeched in the parking lot and Eddie jumped out of the car and came running over. "You're still here," he said, out of breath. "I was afraid I'd miss you."

"What is it, Eddie?" asked Archer.

"The Yankees want to do a press conference."

"A press conference?" asked Louie.

"Yeah, with the dogs."

"With the dogs?" asked Sally.

"Why?" asked Archer.

"They say they're not getting enough good press," said Eddie.

"So what?" said Sally.

"They said if they aren't going to get some good press for doing this game, they don't want to do it."

"That's stupid."

"When do they want to do the press conference?" asked Louie.

"Right now."

"Right now?"

"Yeah, they want a big press conference, with all the reporters and TV cameras and everything," said Eddie.

"I'm not sure about this," said Sally, shaking her head.

Eddie replied, "It'll be easy. They'll ask a few questions and we'll be out of there. In and out, no big deal."

"But the dogs . . ." said Louie.

"Listen, they're looking for a reason to cancel, so if we don't do the press conference, they'll call off the game," said Eddie. "It's as simple as that."

The kids looked at each other and then at Archer, who shrugged. "Let's go."

"You're not putting those dogs in my car," said Andrea as the kids stuffed the dogs into her car. She gave in. "Oh, well, there go the leather seats."

An hour later, they pulled up to Yankee Stadium, the kids and all the dogs, in a caravan of cars and vans. Archer drove Louie, Sally, and their dogs in his Ferrari. Others came with Eddie and Andrea in the Mercedes, and a few parents brought the rest. The press conference was set for five o'clock. They got there moments before five and made their way in a giant gaggle of dogs and kids to the Yankees press room. When they opened the door, a crush of reporters rushed them—like a hundred, maybe more, with TV cameras and big flashy lights on the end of stand-up poles.

"Uh-oh," said Louie.

"You can say that again," said Sally.

"Come on," said Archer. "I've done this before."

Archer led them through the crowd to the front of the room, where a small stage had been set up. A folding table was on the stage. The kids sat down behind the table, and, still on their leashes, the dogs slid under the table. Then the reporters jammed in, the cameramen pushed in, and the lighting guys shoved their lights on stands as close as they could to the dogs.

"Be careful," warned Louie, after a cameraman stepped on Pearl's paw and she squealed.

"Sorry," said the cameraman, who didn't seem sorry at all. The dogs growled at them.

Al entered, pushing Mimi in her wheelchair, and they found a spot in the back. Mimi looked worried. Eddie and Andrea stood to one side. Maggie Hart from the *New York Post* stood next to them, flipping her pad open. Mr. Park came in, holding his brown paper bag filled with treats for the dogs. The room was hot. Louie shook his head, looking out at the chaos.

The doors opened, and Fritz, Andy, and Paul entered, wearing Yankee hats with their suits and ties. They took their seats at the table next to the kids, pulling the microphones closer.

"Okay, okay, settle down," said Fritz to the reporters and cameramen. "This is a first for Yankee Stadium, and I'd like to say, this place is really going to the dogs."

The room erupted in laughter, while the kids petted their dogs to keep them calm.

"Okay, let's get going, who's first?" said Fritz. The reporters jumped up, waving their arms and shouting,

"Over here. Here, here." Fritz picked out a reporter. "You," he called out.

"Good afternoon," said the reporter, rising, as the room quieted down. "I'm from Channel 8, and I have a question." You could hear a pin drop as everyone waited for the first question. "What do the dogs eat before each game?" he asked.

"Coca-Cola and pretzels," said Louie.

"And gelato," added Sally. "They love gelato."

"You," said Fritz, pointing to another reporter, a woman from Channel 6.

"How did the dogs learn to play baseball?" she asked.

Sally took this one. "Well, when they were pups, they started playing Tee-ball. Then came Little League, then Pony League, then high school ball. And then they were drafted into the minor leagues," Sally said. Most reporters scribbled it down like she was serious. "Wow," said Sally, shaking her head.

"Ah, you," said Fritz, pointing to a reporter.

"Do the dogs give autographs?" he asked.

"Sorry, they charge for autographs," said Louie, smiling.

Pushing in even more, the reporters shouted questions all at once, waving their arms, yelling, pushing closer and closer to the dogs. The dogs let out a slow growl.

"Get back," yelled Louie. "Get back."

But they pushed in even further, and the dogs growled louder.

"Stop it," yelled Maggie Hart from the back, but no one heard her. They didn't stop—they pushed in even closer. Chester growled a warning.

"Get back," shouted Louie. "Get back."

"You're scaring the dogs," yelled Sally.

"You stop," yelled Mr. Park, coming forward.

When one reporter stuck his camera in the Bulldog's face, Bull snapped at him.

"Mangy mutt," said the reporter, holding his hand. "He bit me."

"He is not a mangy mutt," shot back Chuck angrily. "You scared him."

Pearl's leash got tangled around a reporter's leg. "Hey, cut that out," he yelled, losing his balance. He caught himself and kicked Pearl, who let out a yelp, and that scared all the dogs, who started running in circles, their leashes getting even more tangled. Bull circled a pole, with a giant burning light on top—wrapping his leash around it. As he pulled away, it teetered and toppled over.

"Look out!" screamed Louie.

The light pole fell and crashed into Chester's leg, and he let out a yelp. Louie jumped off the stage, pushed back the reporters, and grabbed Chester. His leg was bleeding.

"Look what you've done." He lifted him up. "Get back," he yelled. The cameras blocked his path. Al and Maggie and Mr. Park came forward and pushed back the reporters.

Donut and Pal the Great Dane got loose from their leashes and knocked over another light pole, sending it crashing to the floor.

"Get out of my way," yelled Louie, holding Chester across his chest with both arms. "He's hurt."

Chapter Twenty-Three
ON THEIR OWN

"It's not broken, but it's badly sprained," said the sandy-haired veterinarian called in to treat Chester's leg. "And the cut will heal just fine."

"Can he play in the game?" asked Eddie anxiously.

"No, I'm afraid not," said the vet. "The leg won't heal in time. He needs to stay off it."

"There isn't going to be a game," Louie said, firmly.

They were standing in the hallway outside the press room, Archer, Maggie, Al, Mimi, Mr. Park, and all the kids and all the dogs.

"No game?" asked Eddie. "What are you talking about?"

"The game is off."

"I'll wrap his leg and bring him out," said the vet, who disappeared down the hall carrying Chester.

"What do you mean, the game is off?" demanded Eddie.

"There won't be a game," said Louie.

"We have to play."

"We're not playing and that's final," said Sally.

"Why?" asked Eddie. "Why aren't we playing?"

"Look at them," said Sally. The dogs were huddled in the corner—Pal on his belly with his head on the floor, Bull growling, Donut shaking uncontrollably, Pearl whining, Champ's teeth chattering, and the rest looking like they just wanted to go home.

"That's why," said Sally.

"But the whole country will be watching," said Eddie. "They want a game."

"I know they want a game," said Louie. "But there isn't going to be one."

"We can't just call it off," he insisted.

"Mr. Antonetti, we may want to play, but *they don't*," said Louie, gesturing towards the dogs. "They're just doing this for us."

Just then the door opened, and the vet carried Chester, with a bandage on his leg, into the hall and set him down. It hurt so much he could hardly stand on it. He lifted his bad leg and looked at Louie.

"It's okay, boy," he said. "We're going home."

"Just one game," pleaded Eddie.

"No," said a voice. They looked over. It was Dexter Archer. "The kids are right. The game's off. That's final."

"Sorry, Mr. Archer," said Sally, sadly.

"All right," said Eddie, with a sigh, "I'll tell 'em."

Eddie walked over and opened the door to the press room. The reporters rushed at him, like a stampede of cattle, crowding around. "I'm here to make an announcement," he said. "The game between the New York Yankees and the Bronx Barkers has been called off. That is all." He slammed the door shut, over the shouts of the reporters. Andrea came over to him.

"You did good, Eddie," she said.

"Yeah," he said, slumping. "It was good while it lasted."

Al drove the pickup home, with Mimi in the passenger seat and Louie in the back seat, holding Chester in his lap.

"How's he doing?" asked Mimi.

"He's hurt."

In the driveway, Louie carefully lifted Chester out of the truck and carried him inside the house to the kitchen, where he put him down and got him his dinner. Chester ate lying on his side but managed to eat it all up. Whenever he tried to sit up, he put pressure on his leg, and yelped in pain.

"Come on, boy," said Louie, "I'll carry you." He carried him up the stairs to his room. Opening the door with his shoulder, he put Chester on his dog bed, sliding it over so it was right next to his bed. Then he got undressed and climbed into bed. "You'll be okay," he said. Chester's tail thumped on the floor in a steady rhythm.

"Well, boy, you coulda been a star—like Joe DiMaggio or Mickey Mantle or Babe Ruth. You! Chester. At Yankee Stadium. And you couldn't care less, could you, boy?" Chester thumped his tail on the floor even harder. "It's okay, boy. Now go to sleep."

He flicked off the light. For a moment, it was quiet in the room. Then Louie started talking in his announcer voice, *"Chester sets, and there's the pitch. He swings. It's a line drive to center. Chester's off. He rounds first and slides into second for a double. And the crowd goes wild."* He made the *ahhhhhhh* sound of the cheering crowd. He closed his eyes with visions of Chester standing on second, the crowd cheering, his head high, Chester of the Bronx Barkers. The last thing he said, as he was drifting off to sleep, was "Don't worry, boy, you don't have to play if you don't want to."

The morning light cut through the window into his room in a great streak. Louie woke up. He just lay there, thinking for a while, till something made him pick his head up and look around.

"Chester?"

He looked down at the dog bed. It was empty.

"Where are you, boy?"

Chester was gone. Throwing a baseball cap over his messy hair, Louie dressed quickly. He went downstairs past the empty kitchen, through the living room, and out the back door to check if he was in the backyard. "Chester," he called, but he wasn't there.

"Hm," he said. So, he went back into the house and out the front door, onto the street. He looked both ways. No sign of him. "Chester," he called. "Where are you, boy?"

Sally suddenly appeared from down the street, along with Cara, Chuck, Ron, Juan, Donna, and all the others.

"Chester's gone," Louie said.

"So's Marmalade," said Sally.

"So's Donut."

"So's Bull."

"And Bernie."

"They're all gone, all the dogs."

"Where'd they all go?" wondered Sally.

Louie thought for a moment and then it hit him. "Come on," he yelled, taking off down the street, and the kids ran after him.

Full speed they ran down Bayside Avenue, over to Grant, past Mr. Park's market, and into Van Cortland Park. Louie led the way. He ran until he reached the backstop fence and pressed his face against it. Sally hit the fence a moment later and pressed her face against it too, followed by Juan and Ron and Cara and all the others, arriving one by one, pressing their faces against the backstop, looking through it out onto the baseball field. And for a moment no one could speak, not a word, not a sound—they just stared and blinked hard, not believing what they were seeing.

"It can't be," said Cara.

"It's unbelievable," said Veronica.

"It's incredible," said Ron.

"It's sensational," said Donna.

"They're…," said Juan.

"They're playing…," said Chip.

"Baseball," said Louie. "On their own."

And sure enough, right in front of their eyes, the dogs, their dogs, Marmalade and Donut and Bull and all the rest of them, their dogs, were out there, on the field playing baseball, all *on their own*.

Marmalade wound up and pitched, and Bernie the Bernese Mountain Dog hit a line drive into left field. Oscar the German Shepherd fielded it and threw to second to hold the Bernie at first.

"Well, whattaya know about that?" said Sally.

"It really is the dogs who play baseball," said Louie.

A loud bark came from the dugout. It was Chester, standing on the top step. He'd seen them. He was wearing his bandage on his leg, but he kept his head high. The dogs heard the bark, saw the kids, and ran in. And the kids ran out and hugged them.

"I guess they really do want to play," said Louie.

"So what do we do now?"

Louie shrugged. "We play the Yankees," he said.

Chapter Twenty-Four
BACK ON THE PROWL

Eddie stood at his office window, eighteen stories up, overlooking Lower Manhattan, thinking about what could have been, holding back tears.

"Don't jump," said Andrea, coming in with some media reports. "You'll ruin your suit."

He said nothing—just walked back to his desk and flopped in his chair, holding his head in his hands. "We were going to play the Yankees," he moaned. "The Yankees!"

"Well, look at it this way," replied Andrea. "Now you can go back to hiding under your desk."

"Very funny."

"You know, we're broke again."

"It wasn't just about the money, or the fame or the adulation," said Eddie. "I loved those dogs. I loved those kids. I didn't care about the money and the fame and the parade down Fifth Avenue—"

"Coulda fooled me."

"Okay, I wanted the parade, but that's all."

"It'll be okay," she said. "But you better call Nike and tell them the deal is off."

"Niiiiiiiiiiike," he wailed.

Her phone pinged, and she looked at the text. "Or you could call them and tell them it's back on."

He stopped for a moment and looked up at her. "What's back on?"

"The game."

"What game?"

"The game," she said, nonchalantly. "The New York Yankees against the Bronx Barkers. Says it right here. It's back on."

"Let me see that," said Eddie, grabbing the phone away and reading aloud. "THE BRONX BARKERS WILL PLAY THE YANKEES BEFORE THE ALL-STAR GAME AFTER ALL, IT WAS ANNOUNCED TODAY. Is this true?" he said, his voice rising "It's back on? Tell me it's back on."

She nodded. "Looks like it," she said. "Guess we're gonna have to go to more stupid baseball games."

"It's on!" yelled Eddie at the top of his lungs. "It's back on!"

"Quiet, or they'll kick us out of the building," said Andrea.

Eddie ran to the window, yanked it open and yelled out, "The game is on. On! The Bronx Barkers are going to play the New York Yankees."

"Eddie, you'll fall out," said Andrea. "Come back in."

He slammed the window shut, came back in, grabbed her and kissed her, a long kiss. When he broke it off, Andrea blinked a few times and said, "Maybe the dogs should play games more often."

"Quick, text Maggie. We gotta tell Maggie."

At Maggie Hart's new office at the *Post*, she was sitting behind her desk while they were moving out her new furniture and boxing up the flowers, as her editor, Max Makes Millions, paced in front of her desk, talking a million miles a minute, as usual.

"Look, Mag, sorry. I'm sorry, I really am, but the dogs aren't playing, so you're outta here," he said. "Sorry I got to fire you, but it was a good run, good stories, good writing, good circulation, but all good things come to an end, and well, your time is up, you're toast, and maybe I can get you a gig covering the Windsor Locks Beavers for the *Hartford Courant*. It breaks me up, really it does, but no dogs, no stories, and no stories, no job."

Maggie shrugged. She was looking out the window as he rambled on. Jobs come and jobs go, she thought, and she had done her best. She wasn't ever going to feel bad about the dog stories.

Two workmen carried out her coffee table, while another took her pictures off the wall, while another boxed up all her flowers.

"Uh, excuse me," said a workman to Maggie. He wanted her chair.

"Oh, sorry," said Maggie, getting up so he could take it.

Max Makes Millions, in his double-breasted grey suit with polka dotted silk square, headed for the door as her cell phone buzzed. "Hart," she answered. She listened and nodded and few times—and then said, "Yeah, yeah, okay, got it," and hung up.

"Who was that?" said Maximilian.

"Nobody."

"Nobody who?" he insisted.

"Just someone calling about the dogs," she said.

"What about the dogs?"

"Nothing, really. Just that the game is back on with the Yankees."

"It's back on?" demanded Maximillian. "Really back on?" She nodded. He turned and yelled to the workmen. "Okay, back, back. Put it all back, all of it." The workmen stopped, shrugged, reversed course and started putting it all back.

Maximilian wheeled on Maggie. "I want eight hundred words by four o'clock, got it? You got that? I'll hold the front page."

"I thought you just fired me?" said Maggie. "Didn't you?"

"Oh, Hart, don't be ridiculous," he shot back. "You're Maggie Hart. No one fires you. Okay, here's the headline: DOGS BACK ON PROWL. Like it? Do you like it? Well, I do. Get on it, Hart. I need it now, now, got that?" He headed for the door as one of the workmen, carrying her flowers, walked back in. "Who told you to take all this stuff out?" he said sharply. "You did," replied the workman. "That's ridiculous," he said. "That's Maggie Hart in there. And she covers the dogs who play baseball!"

Chapter Twenty-Five
FREDDY THE LITTLE BOY

New York was buzzing. The All-Star Game was scheduled for a Tuesday in July, and today was game day—the best of the National League against the best of the American League at Yankee Stadium. The All-Stars had been in town all week, and the *Post* burst its pages with photos of the players at their hotels, eating dinner, going to nightclubs, living it up in the Big Apple. Now the day was here, but before the All-Star game there was another game—the Bronx Barkers against the New York Yankees.

The town loved it. New York was abuzz with talk of baseball—and dogs. The cab drivers talked of nothing else. The game was sold out, and scalpers were getting five hundred bucks a ticket on the street in front of the stadium. And it wasn't just the city—the entire country was watching. And it wasn't just the country watching either—the whole world was watching. The TV feed was going out all over the United States and to over one hundred countries. Everyone wanted to see if these dogs could really play baseball. Latin America. South America. Japan. China. Africa. Europe. Even Mongolia. The whole world would be tuning in.

It was eight o'clock that morning, and the stadium was empty and quiet, when Dexter Archer appeared in the dugout alone, walked out onto the top step, paused for a moment to take it all in, then walked out onto the field—the same field he had played on for twenty years. He stood between home plate and the pitcher's mound, looking up at the empty stadium.

Louie and Sally slid into the dugout. "Look," said Sally quietly and Louie turned and saw Archer standing there. They came out onto the field.

"I didn't know when I'd ever get back here," he said.

"You did," said Sally. "You're here."

"Sorry it's with a bunch of dogs," said Louie.

"Yeah," said Archer, chuckling. "Not the way I thought . . ."

The rest of the kids and the dogs slowly made their way out onto the field, their eyes growing bigger and bigger as they took in the enormous stadium, the tens of thousands of seats mounting skyward.

"Whoa," said Juan.

"Whoa," said Cara.

"Whoooooooooa," they all said.

"We're in Yankee Stadium," said Sally. They stared upwards. Suddenly, there was a commotion coming from the dugout. "You got some visitors," said Archer. They looked over and saw Froggy and his team came striding out onto the field. Louie and Sally got ready for a fight.

"We're not here for that," said Froggy, waving them off.

"You're not?" Sally asked, putting down her fists.

"No, that can wait. We brought you something for the game."

Froggy and his team brought out bundles. Froggy unwrapped the brown paper off his.

"We figured, you're from the Bronx and we're from the Bronx, so we chipped in and got you uniforms," said Froggy.

"But we already have uniforms," said Sally.

"Not for you, stupid, for them," he said, pointing to the dogs.

"For the dogs?" said Louie. "Uniforms for the dogs?"

Froggy and his team opened their packages and pulled out the uniforms. They were perfect little dog jackets with "Bronx Barkers" written in script on the side, and short-brimmed hats to keep the sun out of their eyes. The kids put the uniforms on the dogs, and they fit perfectly, just right to play in.

"You know, Froggy," said Sally, "you're not such a bad guy after all. Even if you have a little trouble with the numbers."

"Just win," he said.

"Right," said Louie. "Just win."

As the morning wore on, huge crowds jammed the gates into the stadium. The marquee outside said: ALL-STAR GAME TODAY. And below that, SPECIAL FEATURE: BRONX BARKERS VS. BRONX BOMBERS. The fans lined up to get in—kids and dads, moms and grandparents, babies and aunts and uncles, fans from all over the country with their team caps—the St. Louis Cardinals, Los Angeles Dodgers, Chicago Cubs, Seattle Mariners, Minnesota Twins, Arizona Diamondbacks, Philadelphia Phillies—hats from every team. The All-Star Game was for everybody. The whole country came to see their favorite players. The crowd surged through the turnstiles, and as they walked past the concession stands, they heard the vendors calling out.

"Get your bobbleheads! Chester Bobbleheads! Get your Chester Bobbleheads!!!"

And right next to the bobbleheads for Clayton Kershaw, Mike Trout, and Miguel Cabrera was one flying off the shelf—*Chester the Labrador.*

"Chester the Labrador Bobblehead," bellowed the vendor. "Get it right here."

Once through the concession stands, the fans walked into the food court, where hungry fans were lining up for Yankee dogs, pizza, ice cream bowls served in tiny plastic Yankee helmets, grilled burgers, root beer floats, and just about anything worth eating, 'cause everyone knows that everything tastes better at the ballpark. Once through the food court, the fans streamed up the ramps and into the stands. Fans were getting there early, not just for the All-Stars, but to see the dogs play.

A certain young boy took his father's hand walking to their seats in the grandstand. He was maybe eight or nine, with sandy blond hair, thick glasses, and a round face, and his name was Freddy. His father held his hand tightly because Freddy had autism and his dad didn't want him to get lost.

"Dad, are dogs really going to play baseball?" Freddy asked his father.

"We'll see, Freddy. We'll see."

Once in the stands, Freddy and the rest of the fans could look out on the infield, which was now being sprayed down with water one last time to keep down the dirt. The crowd was slowly filling the lower decks, the upper decks, the grandstands, the boxes, and the bleachers. Pennants brought from homes across the country flew for every team in baseball—with kids waving them proudly from their seats. Kids, of course, also brought their gloves so they might have a chance at catching a foul ball. Now they sat, pounding the leather, waiting for the game to start.

A sound system blared music all over the ballpark. The Journey song, "Don't Stop Believing," was playing, and when a giant picture of Chester's huge white Labrador head came on the Jumbotron, the crowd laughed and started singing "Don't Stop *Retrieving*" instead.

Maggie Hart hadn't been back to the stadium since she lost the Yankees beat, but she could still make her way to the press box, where she took her seat. The other reporters couldn't help themselves, yelling down to her, "Hey, Mag, is it a team of chihuahuas?" "Whattaya got next, a team of goldfish?" Maggie took it all in stride, opened her notebook, set up her laptop, and looked out on the field. "I hope this goes well," she said to herself. "Or I'll be covering the Sacramento River Cats by tomorrow night."

Outside the stadium, in the parking lot, Al parked his white pickup, lifted Mimi out of the front seat, placed her in her wheelchair and wheeled her into the stadium—past the bobbleheads of Chester, past the food court, into the elevator, up one level, out onto the concourse, and to an open section for wheelchairs behind home plate. He wheeled her up to the railing, and Mimi said, "Closer, please." Al just smiled because they couldn't get any closer. Mimi looked out over the field. "I'm worried about Louie," she said.

"Look! Chester bobbleheads are going like hot-cakes," said Eddie as he entered the stadium with Andrea, both wearing new Bronx Barker baseball caps. They stopped and got two hot dogs for Eddie, one for

Andrea, put on extra relish and mustard, bought some popcorn and two root beer floats, and made their way into the stands—carrying all this stuff. They took their seats behind the dugout. Andrea looked around at the crowd. "Gotta hand it to you, Eddie," she reflected. "All this for a bunch of dogs."

The Yankees were on the field, warming up, but there was no sign of the kids or the dogs.

"Hmmm," said Eddie. "I wonder where they are—the game's about to start."

"I'm sure they're just getting ready."

"Yeah, I guess..."

In the locker room, Dexter Archer changed into his Bronx Barkers uniform, put on his cap, and faced the mirror. "I hope you know what you are doing," he said, taking a deep breath.

He walked down the hall to the kids' locker room. He stopped outside the door and listened. It was quiet inside. He wondered what was going on. He wasn't sure what to make of it. A locker room was always a crowded, noisy place before a game, he knew that from his playing days. But now—he heard nothing. He opened the door and walked in. At first, he didn't see anything or anyone, just empty lockers. He took a few steps, looked around, but no one was there. He walked around the corner and came face-to-face with the kids and their dogs, huddled together silently. And they were still in their street clothes—all bunched up, hugging their dogs.

"Come on," said Archer. "Get on your uniforms. We got a game to—"

He stopped, because something was wrong. The kids said nothing, but their faces said a lot. "Okay, what's going on?" he said gently.

"We . . . we . . . we just aren't sure about this…," said Juan.

"About what?" said Archer.

"About, you know, the game," said Cara.

"We just don't know," said Chuck.

"This could be bad," said Cara. "Real bad."

"We can't play the Yankees," said Ron. "What were we thinking?"

"We could get slaughtered out there," said Donna.

"And look really stupid," said Levar.

"We could be totally humiliated on national TV," said Chip.

"This is being televised?" said Veronica, aghast.

"We could get killed out there," said Ron.

"The whole county will be laughing at us," said Veronica.

"Maybe we should just go home," said Cara.

Archer sat down on the bench next to them. "Sure, you want to go home—we can go home," he said.

"We can?" they all said at once.

"Sure, sure, we can just pack it in and go home."

"Really?"

"Look, I've played in a lot of big games, and it was scary sometimes—"

"Even for you?"

"Sure, even for me. But if you want to quit, we'll just tell 'em the game's off and go home."

"We can do that?" asked Juan.

"Sure," said Archer.

"We're just scared," admitted Ron. And all the kids nodded sadly.

"Sure, we could take a beating out there," said Archer. "But remember one thing—"

Louie cut in. "If you don't play . . ."

"You can't win," said Sally.

"Right," said the Skipper. "If you don't play, you can't win."

Chapter Twenty-Six
THE BIG GAME

"*Who Let the Dogs Out?*" played loudly on the public address system, the music blaring, and the crowd noise growing louder and louder in anticipation of the dogs coming out onto the field. Everyone wanted to see the dogs. "CHEST-ER, CHEST-ER," they chanted, louder and louder until the whole stadium was chanting it.

And then they came out. The kids came out first in their crisp white Bronx Barkers uniforms with cleats and baseball caps—and the crowd roared. Then Dexter Archer came out, his first time in front of a crowd at Yankee Stadium since he retired, and the crowd went crazy. He tipped his cap. The crowd went wild. And then came the dogs.

The first dog out of the dugout was Chester, in his new uniform, with his hat shielding his eyes from the sun. He could barely walk, limping all the way, his leg still bandaged, but he was there. Then came Bull the Bulldog and Pearl the Scottish Terrier, Oscar the

German Shepherd, and Bernie the Bernese Mountain Dog. Hearing the crowd cheering for them, they trotted jauntily onto the field. Marmalade came next, walking slowly like a pitcher should, head down, stepping over the chalk on her way to the mound. Then came Donut the Mutt, a scraggily thing with wiry hair sticking straight up. She heard the crowd, perked up, and ran the bases. The crowd cheered for her as she crossed home plate.

Champ the Collie and Pal the Great Dane came last, trotting out to the outfield together. The kids joined them on the field, and the crowd roared with delight to see them in their crisp white uniforms. Archer nodded, and they all tipped their caps to the crowd. The Yankees came out onto the field, watching with amazement as the dogs whipped the ball around in warmups.

In the booth, the play-by-play announcer took his seat in front of the microphone. He was a handsome older man who knew his way around a broadcast booth. Clearly, he had been there before. Dressed in a natty sports jacket and grey slacks from Carroll Custom in Beverly Hills, wearing a powder-blue shirt and an LA Dodger tie, he had a voice that everyone knew around the world. His light went on, and he was on the air.

"Well, well, well, it's the All-Star game here at Yankee Stadium," he said on air, "with the game scheduled for a few hours from now, but first we're to be treated to a very special event, a charity game between the Yankees and a team made up entirely of dogs. That's right, folks, dogs, canines, Fido, man's best friend. And from what people tell me, these dogs can really play. But we'll see, as the game is about to start. I'm Ben Tully, and these dogs have hounded me, pardon the pun, out of retirement to call the most unusual baseball game I've ever called, the New York Yankees versus the Bronx Barkers."

The dogs were warming up. The outfielders—Champ, Oscar, and Pal—threw the ball around and caught fly balls. Every time they caught a fly ball, the crowd cheered, as if it was a major accomplishment. Marmalade went to the mound and lobbed a few pitches to Bernie behind the plate. Bull went to third base, Donut to shortstop, Pearl to second, and Gabby the Bassett Hound, who took Chester's place at first base, threw grounders to the infielders, which they fielded and threw back.

"These dogs sure look like they know what they're doing," said Ben Tully . "Oh, boy, this could really be something. I've gotta see this."

Chester, unable to play, his leg still bandaged from the accident at the press conference, stood proudly on the top step of the dugout, watching his team warm up, barking encouragement to the other dogs. Louie gave him a hug. "You'll get 'em next year," he said. Chester wagged his tail.

Walking out onto the field with Sally, Louie scanned the stands for his parents. He saw his mother first, in her wheelchair, with his father standing there next to her, waving to him. "There they are," he said, waving back.

"Look," said Sally, pointing to the Jumbotron. It said: MONEY RAISED FOR SPINAL CORD OPERATION, $0.

"Looks like we got a long way to go," said Louie.

"Look, there's Eddie and Andrea," said Sally, "up in the stands."

"And there's Maggie, in the press box," said Louie, waving to her.

"And Mr. Park. Hello, Mr. Park," they yelled.

"Come on, sound check," said Louie. They ran to the dugout to check the loudspeakers and microphones to see if the dogs could hear the whistles.

"Let's try it," said Sally.

"Okay," said Louie. He whistled into the microphone, and the sound went out over the crowd noise all over the park, so even Pal in deep center heard it and perked up.

"Guess it works," said Sally.

Back in the booth, Ben Tully said, "Now, this is something I never thought I'd see, a team made up entirely of dogs. Well, what do you know about that? There's something new every day."

When the Yankees took the field to warm up, they got an ovation. The kids stopped and stared, mouths dropping open. It was one thing to say you're playing the Yankees, another to see them there, up close. They were so . . . larger than life, larger than any ballplayer these kids had ever seen.

"Look, it's —" said Louie, as the Yankee shortstop whacked a ball in batting practice.

"And look," said Sally, as her favorite player caught a fly ball and whipped it into home.

"And the Yankee catcher," said Juan, as he squatted behind the plate.

"And second base," said Donna, as the second baseman speared a grounder.

"Yep," said Louie. "It's the New York Yankees."

"Uh-oh," said Sally.

"You can say that again." They laughed.

And then, out of the dugout, came Tubby Jackson, the notorious Yankees manager, the toughest, meanest, ugliest, dirtiest, angriest, scariest manager to ever manage a baseball team anywhere. His face said, *I don't like you, and I don't like anyone who likes you.* He was wiry thin, like a bundle of bones, with salt-and-pepper hair, a pencil moustache, and a face like a bird of prey. His eyes were narrow, black, shifting. He had big ears, floppy-like, and a chin that jutted out as if it were coming for you. He took the field, paced five steps, turned his head, and spit.

"Uh-oh," said Sally.

"You can say that again," said Louie.

"I played for Tubby," said Archer, coming up behind them. "He's bad to the bone."

Tubby walked around on the infield grass, wheezed and hacked up another lunger, which he spit onto the grass. His mouth twitched a few times, his nose went up and down, then he sneered up at the crowd like he was getting a root canal and spat again.

"Dogs," he said out loud. "After all these years, I gotta play dogs!"

The umpire came out and swept home plate. Then he turned to both dugouts and called, "Let's see 'em," and the two managers met at home plate with their lineup cards.

"Tubby," greeted Archer.

"Arch," greeted Tubby.

"You're looking good," said Archer.

"No, I look terrible and I know it, but at least I'm not managing a bunch of dogs."

"You haven't seen them play yet."

"I don't need to see them play," Tubby replied. "They're dogs."

"Cards," demanded the umpire.

Reaching into their back pockets, Tubby and Archer pulled out their lineup cards and handed them over.

"Who's leading off, the Bulldog?" snarled Tubby.

"Bull's in the five spot," replied Archer calmly. "Collie leads off."

Tubby shook his head in disgust and spit. "You got some real dogs there, Arch, if you know what I mean."

"You won't be saying that by the second inning."

"There won't be a second inning," said Tubby. The two men were now nose-to-nose.

"Okay, break it up," said the ump. "Play hard, play fair, and no rough stuff, got it? Get it, ruff stuff?"

"Heard it before," said Archer.

"Just stop the game when it gets out of hand," said Tubby to the ump.

The umpire leaned in and whispered to them both, "Okay, my kids are watching and we have two dogs at home, so let's have a good game."

"You gotta be kidding me," sneered Tubby. "Come on."

The public address announcer filled the park. "Tonight's national anthem will be sung by the dog whisperer himself, Cesar Millan."

When the dogs heard that, their ears perked up, their faces turned to the outfield, their tails started wagging wildly. Cesar Millan came out of the stands and walked to the center field. When the dogs saw him, they bolted.

"Where they going?" said Archer, as they tore off.

"To see Cesar," said Sally calmly.

"Who's Cesar?" said Archer. Sally and Louie looked at him, like *are you kidding?*

"What? I never heard of him," he said.

"Oh, say can you see," Cesar sang, and the dogs gathered around his feet. *"By the dawn's early light . . . what so proudly we hailed . . ."* One by one the dogs started to sing along, joining Cesar with howls, yelps, whines— dog singing—until they were all singing the "Star-Spangled Banner," all ten of them, in a choir of dogs. When they got to the end, *"Home of the brave,"* the dogs let out one final howl, ending in a crescendo of singing dogs.

"Plaaaaaay ball," yelled the umpire.

"Dogs don't play ball," yelled back Tubby.

Chester limped his way up and down the dugout. "Sorry, boy," said Louie. Chester let out three loud barks.

"That's the spirit, Chester," said Archer.

"I thought there was no barking in baseball," said Sally.

"Well," said Archer, "there are exceptions. And he's one of them."

"And the Yankees take the field," said Ben Tully on air. "And the Bronx Barkers are coming to bat."

Archer gathered all the kids and dogs together in the dugout. "Okay—dogs, play hard. And kids—whistle loud," he said.

"Very inspirational," said Sally. "Got anything else?"

"Yeah, win."

"Right," said Sally and Louie together.

Out of the dugout came Champ the Collie, the first batter up for the dogs. When the crowd saw the dog dragging the bat tied to her tail, they went nuts and cheered her all the way to the batter's box. The Collie got set, took a few practice swings, and the game got underway. Arnold Rappoport, the Yankee pitcher, threw the first pitch, a fastball.

"Striiiiiiiiiiiiike," yelled the umpire.

The Collie got set, and Rappoport threw another smoker.

"Striiiiiiiiiiiiike," said the ump.

Champ the Collie stepped out and looked back for Levar, who nodded to her. She stepped back in. The next pitch was a curveball, and Champ heard the whistle, waited on it, and hit a hard ground ball into the hole at short. The shortstop, Gaston Martinez, ran hard to his right, snared it backhand, and threw it to first to get the Collie out by a step. But the crowd thought it was great, a real play, and cheered Champ going back to the dugout.

"It's just a bunch of dogs," yelled Tubby, and he spit.

Gabby the Bassett Hound came up next and hit a comebacker to the pitcher for the second out. "Okay, see, it's easy," yelled Tubby. "It's just a bunch of stupid dogs."

Oscar the German Shepherd was up next, took two called strikes, and then hit a line drive to left center that rolled all the way to the wall. Oscar made it easily to second, and a whistle from Juan held him up there.

"What the hell are you doing?" yelled Tubby to his pitcher. "You can't even pitch to a German Shepherd?" The pitcher put his arms out, like *what do you want from me, I've never pitched to a dog before.* "Get back in there," yelled Tub, "and smoke 'em."

Batting cleanup, Bernie the Bernese Mountain Dog trudged slowly to the plate, dragging the bat attached to his tail behind him in the dirt. He got set in the batter's box and spun around and took a few practice swings. Then came the pitch. He heard the whistle, spun hard— the bat came off the dirt and connected solidly with the ball. It flew into right field. It climbed as it went, so it looked like it might go out for a home run, but it hit the top of the wall and fell back onto the warning track. Oscar came around to score, and Bernie flew around second and raced for third. He heard the whistle, slid hard into third, and beat the throw.

"Saaaaaaaaaaaaaaaafe," yelled the ump, spreading out his arms.

"Well, what do you know about that?" Ben Tully told his listeners. "A triple! The Bronx Barkers have taken the lead, one to nothing, with a man, or I should say a dog, on third."

"What the—?" yelled Tubby.

Pal the Great Dane came up next, hitting a long fly ball that went foul at the last minute, or it would have been a home run. He took a strike and then swung hard at the next pitch and missed for strike three.

"After the first half-inning of play, it's Barkers 1-Yanks coming up," said Ben Tully. "We'll be right back, after this commercial break from Beanie's Biscuits for Dogs."

The dogs took the field—Pal the Great Dane in center, Oscar the German Shepherd in left, Champ the Collie in right, Pearl the Scotty at second, Donut the Mutt at short, Bull the Bulldog at third, Gabby the Bassett Hound at first, Bernie the Bernese Mountain Dog behind the plate, and slowly walking to the mound, Marmalade the Whippet.

The second baseman, Morgan, led off for the Yanks. As he walked to the plate, Marmalade threw some warmups and the pitches looked pretty good. He turned back toward the dugout.

"What's the matter with you?" yelled Tubby. "You can't get a hit off a dog?"

Morgan got set in the batter's box, a little uncomfortable because, though he had hit thousands of times, this was his first time facing a Whippet. Marmalade looked in, got the sign from Bernie, wound up, and pitched a fastball, low, just catching the inside part of the plate.

"Striiiiiiiiiiiiiiiiiiiike," yelled the ump.

Morgan stepped out and looked over at his manager, like *you gotta be kidding me.*

"Give me a break," yelled back Tubby. "It's a dog."

He stepped back in. Marmalade wound up and pitched. He swung. Ben Tully called it: "Morgan drives one into right field and he rounds first, then heads back to the bag. The Yanks have a runner on base in the first with nobody out."

"Now we're talking," yelled Tubby. "Get this over with."

Chuck Garner came up, took some warm-up swings, settled in, and waited. Marmalade got the sign, wound up, and pitched. Garner hit a hard ground ball to second. Pearl let the ball hit off her chest, fly up in the air, then right into her Fling Ball basket. She spun, sent a rocket to second, where Donut, covering second from her shortstop position, caught it, flipped it up into her basket, spun around and sent a rocket throw to Gabby at first, beating Garner at first by a step. The crowd went out of their minds.

"Got him," called Ben Tully on the radio. "Now I've seen everything—a four-six-three double play executed perfectly by a Scottish Terrier, a Mutt, and a Bassett Hound. Now, that's something you don't see every day."

In the Yankees dugout, the pitching coach came up behind Tubby. "This ain't gonna be as easy as we thought," he said.

"They're dogs," replied Tubby. "Dogs!" He spit.

"Just sayin'," said the pitching coach, wandering off.

From the Barker dugout, Archer yelled, "Take that, Tubby."

At the end of the first inning, the scoreboard read: Barkers 1-Yankees 0. The Barkers came up in the second but did not score. The Yankees came up in the bottom of the second and got a runner on but couldn't bring him home. And so the Barkers came up in the top of the third inning still leading.

Pal the Great Dane walked slowly to the plate. On the third pitch, Chip whistled into the loudspeakers, and Pal laid down a perfect bunt along the third baseline. Pal, the fastest dog on the team, raced for first. The Yankee third baseman ran in, bare-handed the ball, and threw a bullet to first. Dirt went flying as Pal galloped down the first-base line, and the ball landed in the glove just as Pal's paw hit the base at the same time.

"Saaaaaaaaaaaaaaafe," yelled the ump. In a flash, Tubby was on the field, arguing the call with the ump and demanding a review. So the umps gathered and looked at the play again and again on instant replay with their headphones on. When the home-plate ump took off the headphones, he made the safe sign.

"You gotta be kidding," yelled Tubby. "Dogs can't play baseball."

"Looks like they do," yelled Sally from the dugout.

Donut the Mutt, up next, hit a ground ball up the middle. But Morgan got over and snared it. He only had a play at first as Pal slid into second. One out, one on. Bull the Bulldog was up next. Chuck attached the bat to his tail, and he walked slowly up to the plate, stared the pitcher down, and climbed into the batter's box, getting real close to the plate while taking his practice swings.

"Hey, he's crowding the plate, he's crowding the plate," yelled Tubby from the dugout. True enough, Bull the Bulldog was setting up as close to the plate as he could. "Time," called Tubby. He walked out to the mound to talk to Rappoport. The Yankee infielders joined him for a conference on the mound.

"The Bulldog's crowding the plate," said Tubby.

"So?" said the pitcher.

"So, brush him back," said Tubby, like he was talking to an idiot.

"You want me to brush back a dog?" said Rappoport.

"Skipper, I'm not sure about this," said the shortstop, Gaston Martinez.

"You can't brush back a dog," said Gavin Chavez, punching his catcher's mitt.

"Hey, who's the manager here?" said Tubby. "I say, brush him back. So, brush him back."

"Okay," said the pitcher, sighing. "You're the boss."

Tubby went back to the dugout. Rappoport looked in for the sign, then thought better of it and looked over at Tubby, who looked at him with fire in his eyes, motioning for him to get on with it. Resigned, Rappoport looked in for the sign, got it, and straightened up. He wound up and threw a fastball right at the Bulldog. Now dogs know how to do a lot of things, but how to get out of the way of a hundred-mile-an-hour fastball coming right at them is not one of them. Bull just stood there, watching it come at him. It hit him in his midsection with a wicked *thwap*. Bull let out a squeal, teetered for a moment, and fell over onto his side. A hush came over the crowd, and the stadium went silent. Bull just lay there, not moving, and the whole stadium held its breath. Archer and all the kids came out of the dugout.

"Is he dead?" asked Freddy, the boy in the stands sitting with his father.

"I don't know," replied his dad.

Then Bull lifted his head. "Ohhhhh," the crowd groaned in relief. Bull rose shakily to his feet and staggered around. The pitcher Rappoport looked away, shame on his face. He had hit him intentionally, and everyone knew it. Louie looked over at Archer for the *okay*, and Archer nodded. Louie whistled, not just any whistle but *the* whistle. And all the dogs in the dugout took off onto the field and went straight after the pitcher.

Rappoport took one look at the dogs coming for him—and turned around and ran. He ran past second base and into right field, with the dogs snapping at his heels. He ran in circles, trying to shake them off, but the dogs would not be shook. Pearl and Bernie snapped at his butt and got real close, so Rappoport took off towards the stands, with all the yapping dogs in hot pursuit. The dogs closed in as he got to the railing, so he vaulted into the crowd, where the fans caught him and broke his fall. The dogs barked at him over the railing. The home-plate umpire fought his way through the dogs and jerked his thumb at Rappoport.

"You're throwing him out?" screamed Tubby, arriving at the rail. "You can't do that."

"I just did," snarled the ump. "Nobody hurts a dog on my watch, Tubby."

"Looks like he beaned the bulldog, and now he's paying the price," announced Ben Tully .

Sally looked up at the scoreboard, turned to Louie, and hit him in the arm. "Look," she said.

The Jumbotron said: MONEY RAISED FOR SPINAL CORD SURGERY $24,755.

"Twenty thousand?" asked Louie. "Dollars?"

With some effort, Bull the Bulldog shook it off and walked to first. Chas Beane came in to pitch for the Yankees, and as he warmed up, Archer yelled over to Tubby, "You ain't gonna win that way, Tubby."

"Try me," replied Tubby.

As Bull reached first, the Yankee first baseman, Jake Acheson, leaned down and said, "Hiya, Pooch." Bull looked up at him and gave him a big, wet kiss. The crowd went "ahhhhhhhh" and started chanting, "BULL—BULL—BULL."

It was probably a good thing that the next three dogs didn't get a hit, because Bull was hurt and couldn't run. The Barkers came off the field still leading 1–0.

Marmalade started to tire in the fifth inning, and Acheson lifted a 2–0 pitch into the right-field bleachers for a home run and trotted around the bases to tie the score at one run apiece.

"Uh-oh," said Louie.

"You can say that again," said Archer. They both looked up at him. "What?"

"That's our line," said Sally.

Gianni Jacobson came up next, lifting a fly ball to left field that cleared the fence by forty feet for a home run. He rounded the bases to make the score 2–1 Yankees.

"Well, with two pitches and back-to-back home runs, the Yankees have taken the lead and put the dogs in the doghouse, if you get my drift," said Ben Tully on air.

In the seventh inning, Oscar hit a single to right. He took his lead off first. "Send him," said Archer.

Louie gave the steal sign, and Oscar was off on the first pitch. Dirt went flying as he dug for second. Chavez's throw was a bit high. Oscar heard the whistle and slid in under the tag.

"Saaaaaaaaafe," yelled the ump.

With a perfect sacrifice down the right-field line, Donut the Mutt bunted him over to third, and Bernie the Bernese Mountain Dog came up to bat. He hit a high fly to deep center field. Franklin got under it and made the catch. Oscar tagged up and raced for home, easily beating the throw to tie it up, 2–2.

"Well, I'll be," said Ben Tully to his listeners. "These dogs, no matter what happens, have shown that they can play baseball, really play baseball, as they have gone toe-to-toe, or I should say toe-to-*paw*, with the New York Yankees."

The Yankees came up in the bottom of the eighth with the score tied. They sent Garner to the plate, and he walloped a double off the right-field wall. Champ the Collie caught up with it and threw to second, but Gardner beat the throw. And then the rally started. Martinez singled up the middle, sending Garner to third. Jacobson tripled, scoring two runs, making the score 4–2 Yankees. Gavin Chavez struck out, and Acheson popped up, and it looked like the Barkers would get out of the inning only two runs down, but Peter Tuchman hit a loop single behind Donut at shortstop and Jacobson trotted home, making the score Yankees 5 Barkers 2.

"Uh-oh," said Sally.

"You can say that again," said Louie.

The Jumbotron read, MONEY RAISED FOR SPINAL CORD SURGERY, $38,453.

So, the Barkers came up in the top of the ninth inning, down by three runs. Oscar the German Shepherd was up first, hitting a ball to left field that looked like it would drop in. But Bert Radman made a shoe-string catch, robbing him of a base hit. Oscar came trotting off the field, head down. "It's okay, boy," said the team.

"Two more outs," yelled Tubby, spitting again. "And this is over with."

Bernie came up with all that Bernese Mountain Dog power and swung hard three times—and missed. "Striiiiiiiiike three," yelled the ump. Bernie walked back to the dugout. Sally gave him a treat.

"Two outs," yelled Tubby.

The dogs were down to their last out. Pal the Great Dane came up and got two quick strikes, then saw four balls go by and walked.

"Okay," said Archer, "he's on."

Donut came up and hit the first pitch in the hole between short and third for a single. The dugout went crazy.

"Okay, two on," said Archer. "We've got a rally going."

Pearl the Scotty came up, looked over the field, stepped in, and Donna saw the third baseman playing back. She gave two short whistles, and Pearl bunted down the third-base line. The race was on. Pearl ran for first. The third baseman ran in from third, seized the ball and threw sidearm to first. Pearl's paw hit the base just ahead of the throw.

"Saaaaaaaaaaaaaaaaaafe," yelled the first base umpire.

"Bases loaded," said Archer, clapping his hands. "Okay, who's up?"

"Bull's up," said Chuck, holding the Bulldog in his lap. "But he's hurt."

"Hurt?"

"He's hurt, Skipper. He can't bat. Look at him." Bull tried to get up. "He's hurt from that pitch that hit him," said Chuck.

"But we got nobody else," said Archer. "He's got to bat."

A hush fell over the dugout. Bull gathered all this strength and got up on two legs, then four legs—then fell over.

"He can't, Skipper," said Chuck. "He's hurt."

"Then . . . we'll have to forfeit," said Archer, looking down.

"Forfeit the game?" exclaimed Sally.

"Yeah," said Archer. "We have no one else to pinch hit."

It sank in. The game was—over. The bases were loaded in the ninth inning, with two outs and the game on the line, and they had no one to bat. There was nothing they could do. They hung their heads.

"You're a bunch of losers," yelled Tubby, from his dugout.

The umpire stuck his head into the dugout. "You gonna bat or what?" he asked.

"We may have to—"

"Wait," said Sally.

Chester was getting up. He made his way, limping, over to the bat rack. He picked up a bat, took it between his teeth, and walked over to Louie, who looked down with concern.

"No, boy, you can't," said Louie. "Your leg."

Chester then limped his way over to Archer. He dropped the bat and barked.

Archer looked over at Louie and Sally. "He can barely walk," said Archer.

Sally shrugged, "What do we have to lose?"

Louie knelt down next to Chester and put his arm around him. "You think you can, boy?" Chester wagged his tail. Louie looked up at Archer, and nodded. Louie lifted Chester into his lap, removed the bandage and slowly fastened the bat to his tail. Their eyes met. "Go get 'em, boy." Chester rose, limping heavily, and walked out onto the grass.

"Well, what do you know about this?" said Ben Tully from the booth. "It's bases loaded, ninth inning, and the Barkers are sending up the Labrador, and the poor pooch can barely walk."

"Go ahead, send up your cripple," yelled Tubby from across the infield.

"He's not a cripple," Louie yelled back. "He's not."

"Take it easy," said Archer. "Let Chester do the talking with his bat."

In the Yankees dugout, the pitching coach came up behind Tubby. "Dole," he said.

"What? Are you nuts?" said Tubby. "You want me to put in my ace against a bunch of dogs?"

"You want to lose to a bunch of dogs?" replied the pitching coach.

"Time," yelled Tubby, and on his way to the mound he tapped his right arm.

"Uh-oh," said Archer, looking on from the dugout.

"What?" said Louie.

Ben Tully said, "Oh, my Lord, looks like he's bringing in Johnny Dole, their ace, to face the Labrador."

"It's Dole," said Archer. "He's the best they got."

Dole trotted in from the bullpen and took eight warm-up pitches, with Tubby standing right behind him on the mound.

"Okay, you got a hundred-mile-an-hour fastball, right?" said Tubby.

"Yeah," said Dole.

"Use it." Dole nodded.

Tubby walked slowly back to the dugout, spitting as he went. Chester stepped into the batter's box, digging his front leg into the dirt and then moving his back leg, the hurt leg, around into position. He took a practice swing and winced in pain.

"Uh-oh," said Sally.

Dole got the sign, checked the runners, and fired a 99-mile-an-hour fastball on the outside corner. Chester swung, missed badly, fell on his bad leg, and yelped in pain.

"He's a loser," yelled Tubby. "Easy out."

Chavez threw the ball back to Dole, who rubbed it up and stepped on the rubber. He got the sign, checked the runners and threw a 101-mile-an-hour fastball. Chester saw it, spun around and swung, missed badly, and fell over onto his side. The crowd went silent.

"He's done," yelled Tubby. "It's over."

Chester couldn't get up, much as he tried. He just pushed his leg around in the dirt and tried again and again to rise. "The dog is a cripple," yelled Tubby.

"He's not a cripple. He's a good dog," yelled Louie, from the top step of the dugout.

"Let me tell you something, kid," Tubby yelled back. "That dog's a loser, and you're a loser and all you kids over there are losers—you got that!"

Chester lifted his head from the dirt and looked over at Tubby, with a bold, harsh stare that said, *you don't talk to him that way*. He stared at Tubby for a long time. Then, slowly, he rose. With one giant effort,

Chester lifted himself up onto four legs. The crowd cheered.

"He can't even walk," sneered Tubby. "Easy out."

"It's okay, boy. Come on back," said Louie. He started to go get him, but Chester turned back to the plate. But this time he walked around to the other side of the plate. Louie watched from the top step of the dugout.

"What's he doing?" asked Archer.

"He's going to bat lefty," said Louie. "So he can use his good leg."

"Can he bat lefty?"

"We're going to find out," said Sally.

Tubby came to the top step of the dugout and yelled out to Dole, "Smoke him." Dole got the ball, looked in for the sign, straightened, checked the runners, wound up and threw a 99-mile-an-hour fastball over the outside part of the plate. Chester's eyes never left the ball. He heard the whistle from Louie, long and low, which meant a fastball outside. He spun around fast, his back leg now working well, and the spin brought the bat up to the ball. *Crack!* He hit a fly ball to right field. Dole's head snapped around as it went by. The right fielder turned and ran back towards the wall. The crowd rose to their feet. The right fielder reached the wall and put his hand on it to steady himself. And with his mitt outstretched he jumped as high as he could.

"It's going, going, going . . .," said Ben Tully. "It's . . ." The whole stadium froze watching the ball and the right fielder stretch his mitt out for it. And the ball sailed just over his mitt and into the right-field bleachers.

"Gone!" called Ben Tully . "A home run! Well, now I've seen everything—a limping Labrador just hit a grand slam off the best pitcher in baseball, and the Barkers have taken the lead."

Oscar trotted in from third and crossed home plate. Donut rounded third and came in to score. Bernie rounded second, rounded third, and crossed home plate to tie the score. Chester limped his way down to first, where first baseman Acheson looked down at him and said, "Nice hit, Pooch." Chester wagged his tail and headed for second. The second baseman, Morgan, looked down and said, "Way to go, boy," and Chester wagged his tail and rounded second.

But then his limp got worse, his leg locked, and he pulled up. He took a halting step and stopped. He took one more pained step and then stopped dead in his tracks.

"He can't make it," yelled Tubby. "He's got to make it on his own, or he's out!"

"I'll go," said Louie.

"No," said Archer, holding him back. "He has to do it himself or they'll call him out."

"Out, out, out," yelled Tubby to the ump. "Call him out."

Chester tried a few more steps, but the pain was too great. He stopped and looked over at the dugout for Louie.

"I don't care if we win," said Louie. "I gotta go to him."

Archer nodded. "Then go," he said.

But just then the Yankee shortstop, Gaston Martinez, leaned over Chester, who was stuck there between second and third base. "Hiya, boy," he said, kneeling down beside him. "How's the leg doing?" He touched it, and Chester winced. "Hmmm, you need to go on injured reserve," he said. He looked up at the third base ump.

"Okay if I help him?" he asked.

The ump thought about it. "His own team can't help him, but nothing says you can't."

So, Martinez picked Chester up, wrapping his arms around the dog's four legs, and started walking towards third base.

"Put that dog down," screamed Tubby. "Put him down."

But Martinez didn't put him down, and instead brought him to third and bent down on one knee so Chester could touch the base with his paw.

"Stop," yelled Tubby. "I said stop!"

Martinez stood up and started down the third-base line towards home, holding Chester. Tubby ran out of the dugout and blocked his way, placing his wiry body in the base path.

"Put down that dog," screamed Tubby. "If you ever want to play another baseball game in your life, put him down."

"He hit it fair and square, Skipper," said Martinez.

"Put that dog down right now or you'll be benched for the rest of your career."

"Skipper, listen, I got kids at home, and they're watching right now, so move aside, and let me go."

Tubby looked at Martinez, saw in his eyes he wasn't going to give up, and stepped aside. Gaston Martinez carried Chester down the line to home plate. Chester looked up and gave him a big lick on the face.

"Now, that's a shortstop," said Archer, watching from the dugout.

"You should know," said Sally.

The kids charged the plate, crowding around, jumping up and down as the Yankee shortstop put Chester down on home plate.

"Well, I thought I'd seen everything, but I've never seen anything like this," said Ben Tully .

The crowd chanted, "CHEST-ER, CHEST-ER." Chester touched the plate with his paw, and the scoreboard changed to Barkers 6-Yankees 5. The crowd rose and gave Chester a standing ovation as he came off the field.

"Take a bow, boy," said Louie. Chester stopped and acknowledged the crowd, letting his head rise. And the crowd didn't stop for more than a minute.

The Yankees came up in the bottom of the ninth inning and loaded the bases with two outs. For a moment it looked like the Yanks would pull it out, but then Sally walked to the mound and had a few words with Marmalade. "What did you say to her?" Archer asked when she got back. "I told her she could have as many hamburgers as she wanted if she got us out of the inning."

"Smart," said Archer, nodding.

And Marmalade threw a fastball to the Yankee batter, who swung and missed. Marmalade got the ball back and threw another pitch. "Strike," called the ump. Marmalade got the ball back, wound up with everything she had, and threw a fastball down the heart of the plate. He swung. And missed.

"Well, it's hard to believe—I wouldn't have believed it myself if I hadn't seen it—but a team made up totally of dogs, the Bronx Barkers, have beaten the New York Yankees," said Ben Tully over the airwaves.

Fireworks went off over the stadium, and all the All-Stars—Clayton Kershaw from the Dodgers, Mike Trout from the Angels, Javier Baez from the Cubs, Carlos Santana from the Indians, and all the rest—came out, tipped their caps to the Barkers, and took selfies with Chester and Marmalade and the other dogs.

Eddie and Andrea stood in the stands, watching as the fireworks explode over center field. "You did it, Eddie," squealed Andrea. "You did it."

"No, they did it, the dogs and the kids. They did it."

In the press box, the reporters looked on as the dogs celebrated, shaking their heads in disbelief. Then, one by one, they mobbed Maggie, shaking her hand and slapping her on the back.

On the field, Fritz, the Yankees GM, walked up to Archer and said, "Okay, okay."

"Okay what?" said Archer.

"Look, anyone who can beat the Yankees with a bunch of dogs can manage for us anytime," said Fritz. "You can start on Monday, Triple A in Cleveland."

"Really? That's great," said Archer. "I won't let you down."

"Think I can get a picture with Chester?" said Fritz. He handed his phone to Sally and put his arm around the Labrador while Sally snapped the picture.

"What about him?" said Louie, looking over at Tubby, sitting alone in the dugout, head down.

"Come on," said Archer, and they walked over to the dugout.

"I lost to a bunch of dogs," said Tubby. "I'll never live this down."

"How about a picture?" said Sally.

Tubby looked up and over at the dogs, raised his arms like *why not?* and said, "Oh, what the heck." He shook Louie's hand and Sally's hand and went over to Chester and all the other dogs and knelt down. All the dogs gathered around Tubby. Sally took the photo. "For my grandkids," he said. "They'll love this."

Mr. Park looked up at the Jumbotron and stood up. He pointed. Others looked. Soon the whole stadium was looking at the Jumbotron. He saw Louie on the field and waved to him. Louie waved back. "Look, look," said Mr. Park. Louie and Sally turned and looked up.

The Jumbotron said: MONEY FOR SPINAL CORD OPERATION: $3,400,279.

"Three million dollars?" exclaimed Louie. "Three million?"

"Louie," said Sally. "Now your mom can have her operation."

Louie scanned the crowd and spotted his mother in her wheelchair—with his father standing by her side at the railing. Louie waved. They waved back. Louie could see her handkerchief, so he knew she was crying.

The sound system started playing the song "Don't Stop Believin'," and the crowd sang, "*Don't Stop Retrievin'*" until everyone joined in, the All-Stars, the Yankees, the kids and even the dogs.

Fireworks went off over their heads. Louie and Sally, with Chester limping along, plus Marmalade, walked together into center field. Chester's huge face appeared on the Jumbotron, with a giant headline: MVD—MOST VALUABLE DOG.

Louie put his arm around Chester. Sally put her arm around Marmalade. Then Louie reached out and put his other arm around Sally—and the four of them, two dogs and a girl and a boy, with their arms around each other, gazed up at the fireworks bursting overhead.

"We did it," said Sally. "We did it."

"You can say that again," said Louie.

Chapter Twenty-Seven
CHESTER'S AUTOGRAPH

After the game, it was right to the ice cream parlor for cones for the kids and cones for the dogs, and even cones for the grownups. Everyone showed up—all the kids, the dogs, the parents, Mimi and Al, Eddie and Andrea, Mr. Park, Maggie Hart, and Dexter Archer and his wife Sarah, who gave him a big hug. Eddie wandered over to Maggie Hart as she sat devouring a dripping chocolate ice cream cone.

"I hear you got the Yankees back," said Eddie.

"Yeah, they offered it to me," said Maggie.

"That's great."

"I turned it down."

"You turned it down?" exclaimed Eddie.

"Yeah, I already got a job," said Maggie. "I'm covering the Bronx Barkers."

She smiled and moved away. Andrea came up to Eddie.

"You're the most famous PR guy in New York, Eddie," she said. "And you're rich."

"About that . . ." he said.

"What?" Andrea asked slowly.

"I kinda . . ."

"What did you do, Eddie?"

"I donated all the money to Louie's mom," he blurted out.

"All of it?" asked Andrea.

"For her operation," he said.

"Oh, Eddie, what am I going to do with you?" And she threw her arms around him.

The door to the ice cream parlor opened, and the little boy Freddy came in with his father—still holding his dad's hand. His father let go and gently nudged the boy forward and Freddy walked slowly across the ice cream parlor and up to Dexter Archer, holding out his program. Archer knelt down next to him. "Hiya, kid. Want an autograph?"

Freddy looked beyond Archer at Chester across the room. Archer turned, saw, and turned back. "Oh, you want *his* autograph?" he said. Freddy nodded. "Okay," said Archer. Freddy walked over to Chester and held out his program for an autograph.

"Wait," said Louie. "I have an idea."

He took Chester's paw and dipped it into his ice cream cone, then planted a perfect ice cream paw print on Freddy's program. "There," he said, "Chester's autograph."

"Thank you," Freddy said. "Thank you, Chester."

The crowd clapped and Chester barked three times, and all the dogs barked three times.

"Are you barking?" yelled the kids together. "Are you barking? 'Cause there's no barking in baseball."

Chapter Twenty-Eight
THE VISITOR

It was six months later, and in the backyard of Louie's house in the Bronx, a baseball game was being played, with Marmalade on the mound, Chester at first, and Pearl at second, Sally at bat, and Louie playing third. Al looked on and Mimi sat nearby in her wheelchair, watching the game. The doorbell rang inside the house, and they all heard it, and Al started to rise.

"I'll get it," said Mimi. She placed her hands firmly on the arms of her wheelchair and pushed herself up until she was standing. She took a step, then another, then walked all the way into the house. Holding the ball, Louie watched her go inside. His father smiled at him.

Mimi walked through the kitchen, through the living room, and to the front door. She opened it. A man was standing there.

"Hello, I'm sorry to disturb you. My name is—"

"I know who you are," said Mimi softly, almost as if she was expecting him. "Come in."

She led the man through the house and out into the backyard. They came out onto the patio and stood there, and one-by-one the kids stopped playing and turned to look. The man was tall, African-American, handsome, and athletic.

"Hello," he said.

"Hello," they all said.

The man cleared his throat. "I'm —."

"We know who you are," said Sally. "We're not complete idiots."

"Well, nice to meet you," said the man.

An awkward silence followed. Then Louie spoke up, "We know who you are, but what we don't know is why are you here."

The man cleared his throat. "Well, I'm here because I wanted to meet you all and the dogs."

"Well, this is Chester," said Louie.

"Hello, Chester," he said.

"And this is Marmalade," said Sally.

"Hello, Marmalade." The man looked at the dogs as if he were expecting a response.

"They can't talk," said Sally.

"Right," he said. "Well, it's like this. I saw the game against the Yankees on TV. I mean, everyone saw the game—the whole country saw the game …"

"Yeah?" said Sally.

"And I was wondering . . ."

"Yes?"

"Would the dogs like to play golf?"

"Golf???" exclaimed Louie and Sally together, wide-eyed, turning to each other in amazement. "Golf!!!"

"Yeah, the dogs who play golf," said the golfer, flashing a fantastic smile. "What do you think?"

Louie's smile burst out. And Sally's, too. They looked at each other, like the friends they were and always would be, and thought *it doesn't get much better than this*.

And Chester barked.

THE END

ACKNOWLEDGMENTS

Several people were instrumental in the publication of this book and I would like to show my appreciation: my editor, Margaret Harrell for helping this book along and believing in it from the beginning; formatter Debbie Lum for giving this book just the right look; Blaine Smith for her amazing attention to detail in copyediting; Laura Chambliss of Studio Yopp for the cover design; Zoe and Eve Buehler for being the first young readers to read the book and for their feedback; editorial associate Sarah Groth for marketing and management; my wife Sheri and family for their encouragement; and John Carroll and the Los Angeles Dodgers for always being there, summer after summer, keeping the flame alive.

A portion of the proceeds from this book will be donated to Little League Baseball.

ABOUT THE AUTHOR

Thomas Louis Carroll is the author of the novels *The Colony* and *The Dogs Who Play Baseball* for young readers. He now lives with his wife Sheri, a miracle-working Educational Assistant, in Santa Fe. He has three fantastic daughters. He has also written screenplays and produced and directed two films, *Big Bad Budget*, seen on PBS stations, and *Who Stole the Tasmanian Devils?* When not writing, Tom is an avid skier, windsurfer, swimmer, and dogsledder, which he does most years in Northern Minnesota.

He can be reached at tom@dogswhoplaybaseball.com

WRITE A REVIEW

Thank You for Reading My Book

Write a review!

If you are so inclined, please help and leave me a review on Amazon, letting me know what you thought of the book.

It means a lot for other readers to hear from those who have read the book.

Thanks so much!

Thomas Louis Carroll

And you can reach me personally at
tom@dogswhoplaybaseball.com

Come and add your name to the email list
and we'll send you the autographed photo
of Chester the Labrador.

To join up, go to
www.DogsWhoPlayBaseball.com

Made in the USA
Monee, IL
29 July 2022